I0198441

SEBASTOPOL TRENCHES.

Sebastopol Trenches

AND

FIVE MONTHS IN THEM.

BY

COLONEL REYNELL PACK, C.B.,
7TH FUSILIERS.

" The path of Duty was the way to Glory !
   *   *   *   *   *
Oh, Statesmen ! guard us, guard the eye, the soul
Of Europe. *   *   *   *   *
Drill the raw world for the march of mind,
Till crowds at length be sane, and crowns be just ;
But wink no more in slothful overtrust !"
   *   *   *   *   *
     " Cannon to right of them,
     Cannon to left of them,
     Cannon in front of them,
     Volley'd and thunder'd ;
     Storm'd at with shot and shell.
       *   *   *   *
     When can their glory fade ?"—   TENNYSON.

LONDON:
KERBY & ENDEAN, 190 OXFORD STREET.
1878.

All rights reserved.

PREFACE.

THE following narrative of Five Months' Life in the Trenches before Sebastopol was written by the late Col. Reynell Pack, from notes taken by him at the time. Written with no attempt to imitate the practised skill of the historian, or to describe with the facile pen of the experienced newspaper correspondent, it is a soldier's plain narrative of a soldier's experience when engaged, for many weeks, in the active duties of camp and trench life besieging the chief seaport of the enemy.

This volume would have appeared immediately after the Crimean campaign, but as it contains strong comments on the capacity and qualifications of certain officers, its publication was deferred till a fitting time arrived for its issue.

The period in the Siege of Sebastopol and the Life in the Trenches more especially described in this volume, have scarcely been presented by any writer other than the professional correspondents of our valued and potential press. Much interest, it is believed, will be taken in the following pages, and more especially at the present moment, when the Eastern Question is again absorbing the whole political attention of Europe,—it is therefore with greater confidence offered for public perusal.

Life in the Trenches was much the same from day to day: actions, sorties, night attacks, fierce bombardment from the forts, a watchful enemy ever on the alert, much peril experienced, many deeply interesting incidents occurring; but the indomitable patience and perseverance of commanders, officers, and men eventually crowned the besiegers with success. No siege of history ever concentrated upon itself so mightily the whole gaze of the civilized world as the Siege of Sebastopol, and whatever illustrates that siege and the character of the combatants engaged therein is of deep general interest.

The Frontispiece is a copy of the Orders and Honours conferred on Major-General Sir Denis Pack, K.C.B., and on his son Colonel Reynell Pack, C.B., and it prefaces this volume for the purpose of shewing that nations recognise gallant and heroic deeds, and are ever ready to honour services loyally discharged. At the same time it may not be amiss to state that these Orders and Honours are all that remain to the present representative of the family in acknowledgment of the services rendered by these gallant officers, who virtually lost their lives in defending their country's honour.

The panoramic sketches are from the pencil of Captain M. A. S. Biddulph, Royal Artillery. They were issued by him at the time of the campaign ; but as their circulation was limited, it is felt that their re-issue in these pages is most appropriate, and thanks are gladly given to their respective publishers for the ready courtesy and kindness with which permission was given for their reproduction.

AVISFORD, 1878.

CONTENTS.

CHAPTER VII.

CHAPTER VIII.

CHAPTER IX.

SEBASTOPOL TRENCHES.

CHAPTER I.

On the 28th of March in the year 1854 War was declared against Russia by the Allied forces of France and Great Britain in defence of the independence of Turkey, and speedily steps were taken to mass the troops of each country in combination on the shores of the Crimea.   This portion of the enemy's territory apparently presented the most vulnerable point for attack, and, as was subsequently proved, the selection was judiciously made.

From the date of the Declaration of War in March

A

no event of great importance, from a military point of view, occurred until the "Army of Occupation" landed on the Crimean shores, in the neighbourhood of Eupatoria and the river Alma, on September 14th ; on the 20th, the ever-memorable battle of the Alma was fought, resulting in the complete rout of the Russians, and triumph of the Allies.

So decisive and complete a victory was not contemplated. Provision had not been made to follow it up by a rapid march on to, and, if possible, into Sebastopol. The opportunity then offered was lost, and the country had to pay the consequent penalty in the heavy loss of men and in the great expenditure of money that followed during many months of the subsequent siege.

On the 17th of October the first fire of our batteries was opened on Sebastopol. The French and English as agreed, on signal given, commencing at 6.30 in the morning, and for about two hours the bombardment and replies from the Russian defences were terrific. Convinced by this time that nothing could divert the Allies from the siege until victory was gained, the Russians strenuously laboured to obtain every advantage possible, and on the 25th of October, in the Valley of Balaclava, was fought the "Battle of Balaclava," when the charge of the Light Brigade took place, than which nothing in the history of war stands out with greater prominence or is marked with nobler courage, bravery, and self-sacrifice than then occurred. The enemy was completely foiled, although in far superior numbers, and retreated as speedily as they were able within their defences.

This attempt was followed up by another on the 5th of November, when, under cover of a dense fog and drifting rain, the Russians stealthily crept up the Inkerman heights. It was a Sunday morning—the church bells were ringing in the city as if for service, and little suspicion was entertained in the Allied camp that the enemy was close at hand, and reckoning on the strong probability of pouncing upon a camp "happily reposing" on a winter's morning.

"Caught napping," as the camp undoubtedly was, the British lion speedily sprung from his lair, and, shaking himself, rushed heroically into the fight, aided by his allies, when the most signal triumph was again obtained, the enemy was driven back in every direction, in many places at the point of the bayonet, suffering fearfully, whilst we also sustained heavy loss at a time when we could ill spare a single man.

The Battle of Inkerman brought us no nearer to the city. The siege continued, and drew on its weary course from day to day with all its terrible associations. November passed, and December followed. Parallels and zigzag trenches now covered the heights in front of the city, and nearly surrounded it. It was at this time—having relinquished our appointment at the Horse Guards in order that we might more actively serve our country—we received orders for the Crimea, and, quickly making arrangements, with the new year we were ready to sail.

A dark winter's morning in the month of January, 1855, ushered in our departure for the Seat of War. We were to embark in charge of drafts of Regiments proceeding by steam ship to Balaclava.

Departures are invariably sad, and this was no exception. Duty and honour struggled with those true feelings of love and affection best known to parents and husbands. The tender links binding us to home were to be dissevered, and man's natural ties were to be held in abeyance in obedience to the calls of our profession.

The thought too could not fail to cross the mind, how few were remaining of those brother officers whose comradeship had been our enjoyment in years gone by! of friends, who had sailed bright with hope and honourable ambition, whose only history, after a few short weeks, was the newspapers' brief record : a shot or a shell had laid them low. Then perhaps the mail brought a kind letter of condolence from a commanding officer, telling a bereaved mother, or wife, or sister, that the son, or husband, or brother had met a soldier's death in gloriously repulsing a sortie, or in dislodging the enemy from a redoubt.

Or possibly a few kindly expressed words of sympathy from our gentle Queen, and all is told. A marble slab in some ancient cathedral, or a more humble monument in the village church proclaims to fond friends that such a one fell nobly in the service of his country and in the cause of freedom in the great struggle of the age ; or maybe he will be only thought of and remembered by a few of the martial spirits of the next generation who embrace the profession of arms.

But the train starts and quickly bears us off. Ere long all feelings are drowned in the calls of duty,

—that stern sense which training and a long career in the army only perfect, and by which discipline is produced :—that sense, so often misunderstood and erroneously called, heartlessness.

Our vessel was a screw steamer of one thousand and forty-five tons, calculated with cargo, when engaged in ordinary traffic, to carry three hundred and fifty-eight deck, and two hundred and thirty-six cabin passengers ; but, altered as she had been for military purposes, she was adapted to convey somewhere about nine hundred men and twenty officers There was dire confusion on board, as those who have seen troops an hour or two after embarkation will readily believe.

Drafts from eleven different regiments were ordered to proceed in her to the seat of war: eight were already embarked, two were expected to arrive shortly, and the remaining detachment was to be taken on board at ———. It was not long before the arrival was announced of the two drafts for which we were waiting. They had started on their march about the same time,—one from the north of England, and the other from a less distant point.

The first had formed part of a distinguished Irish

corps, recently returned from India. Composed principally of men whose habits were unsteady, they, when their regiments previously sailed, had been left at home undergoing punishment, but they were noble old soldiers, fit for any work. It was a strange sight to see their arrival. Many had evidently been drinking—some were very drunk--and all appeared rather unsteady. Prior to marching on board they were drawn up in line, and numbered about one hundred and twenty, as fine fellows as Her Majesty was ever likely to secure, though certainly, in their then state, they were likely to prove dangerous and unruly to the Queen's lieges.

The functionary, who was going through the form of inspecting them and superintending the embarkation, said to a half-drunken rear-rank man, decorated with a riband, " You are no soldier." " No soldier, indeed," replied the Burmese hero, " Faith, your honour may take that to yourself. It is a pity the likes of you talks of 'no soldier,' indeed."

The man was immediately ordered to be arraigned before a court-martial on board, but the unsteady detachment, once embarked, there was no time judicially to try a man for an answer which, although

no doubt "subversive of good order and military
discipline," was produced by an indiscreet and unnecessary observation from a staff-officer. "What's
from the captain but a choleric word is, in the soldier,
sheer mutiny."

During the voyage this detachment behaved as
well as, if not better than, most of the others; and
what a contrast the men presented physically to the
other detachments. They were old, tried soldiers fit
for any service or duty, whilst the other drafts were
mostly undrilled boys fresh from the plough, ignorant
alike of their drill, the first rudiments of discipline,
or attention to personal cleanliness.

As a type of the class of youths embarked under
the denomination of soldiers it may be stated, that
one of the oldest soldiers, out of a draft of probably
one hundred and twenty men, acted as an officer's
servant, and had only been six weeks in the service
from the date of his enlistment.

Having shipped our living cargo our next trial
was to consider applications from most of the nice
young gentlemen gazetted as officers (many in command of drafts), for permission to leave their men
that they might dine and sleep on shore.   "Ce n'est

que le premier pas qui coûte." Of course, if the request of one had been granted it would have been scarcely just to refuse the others ; so, however painful to disoblige mothers, guardians, uncles, and other relatives it was necessary to negative their wishes.

Nothing renders men more discontented than, with plenty of uncooked food on board, to have nothing but the prospect of remaining with empty stomachs. And soldiers are no exception to this rule. With coppers that would not draw it is not surprising cooking was difficult. Instead of the heat warming the boilers, it went downwards and radiated about the surrounding deck. This defect was complained of and repeatedly represented to the staff-officer who embarked us, but it was not remedied ; the presumption was that the want of experienced cooks, and our ignorance as to the proper allowance of air were the causes of the inability to cook our victuals. Be that as it may, the consequences were very nearly most serious.

That afternoon, amidst the cheers of thousands and the counter cheers of the thousand men on board, the ship left the port, the embarking officer having taken no further steps to repair the radical defect of the

coppers, but left us with the consolatory expression,
" God speed you."

Seeing troops embark, even for the colonies, is
always a melancholy spectacle, and nine-tenths of the
never-failing cheers given on such occasions are by
individuals who are wholly ignorant why they utter
such sounds. Still more sad is it to hear the yells of
some hundreds of youths going on active service.
In both cases the reflection arises : how few will
return ! But with the latter there is the additional
thought : how few of the gallant spirits who, it is
presumed, thus testify their willingness to peril life
and limb for their queen and country will return
whole and sound !

It is no hazardous or exaggerated statement that,
of the ninety men composing the draft to which we
belonged, not ten of the rank and file are now serving. Of the officers on board (sixteen in number),
one died, two were killed, five were severely wounded,
and the remainder, with the exception of four, were
slightly wounded. Of the four that escaped, one
sold out, and two were absent for some time from
sickness. The disabled and death losses were undoubtedly severe.

Thus within six months from leaving the shores of England, deducting the three officers who immediately left the army from sickness and resignation, out of a total of thirteen one only escaped unhurt.

With a smooth sea we steamed down channel, anchoring off ———— at daylight. The dinner hour arrived, but no dinner likely to be ready for several hours does not put people in the best of humours. Our coppers would not draw; daily our soldiers' dinners were deferred and could not be ready before a fashionable hour; in many instances tea was postponed until the next morning. Lying quietly at anchor our appetites increased in strength, and endeavours were made to cook a fair Sunday meal. Vain effort ! The heat struck downwards under the deck instead of radiating upwards and heating the boilers, and it was not long before fire was discovered smouldering and smoking between decks.

An experienced officer fortunately happened to be captain of the day, who, without raising unnecessary alarm, reported the matter; the agent of transports, —an energetic, practical seaman—being on board, the fire which, had there been much wind, might have been obstinate, or, if it had occurred at sea would almost certainly have proved our destruction, was easily and happily overcome, but with considerable loss to the detachment berthed between decks immediately in its vicinity.

Dinners, too, were gone for many on that day. Each, however, endeavoured to make the best of what was a bad business. There was probably much inward thankfulness felt by the majority that the threatened calamity did not occur at sea.

At the time the editor of one of the principal local newspapers happened to be on board, who, on presenting a copy of his journal to the commanding officer, said, " I am the editor of this, and also provincial correspondent of the *Times.*" These words were frank, but their consequences were, great civility, little information, and close attention to the proceedings of our unknown friend. He was observed making notes, but returning on shore with the ship's captain, and one of the owners (who came thus far with us), it is surmised the eloquence and persuasion of the two were such that very trifling if any notice of the fire was taken by the *Times.*

Our ship was now hauled alongside one of the hulks ; a portion of the troops temporarily transhipped, and workmen sent to fit new coppers and grates ; after thirty-six hours' labour, night and day, new and effective cooking places were completed. This essential finished, we prepared to bid " Farewell to England."

The heterogeneous nature of our freight produced many inconveniences as to accommodation. Independently of the drafts (upwards of nine hundred men), including the regimental staff, paymasters, quarter-masters, veterinary surgeons, twenty-two in number, we conveyed store-keepers, purveyors, and letter-sorters. Some thought they were entitled to better berths ; others, again, complained of being too closely packed ; nearly all had never before been to sea.

To realize the difficulties attending the management of numerous drafts composed of recruits, with a great proportion of the subalterns and non-commissioned officers wholly inexperienced, one must be placed in such circumstances ; the very sentries ignorant of their duties, and innocently allowing the orders given to be disobeyed ; the impossibility of mustering men in a very crowded ship, or of parading a watch, where there was no space so to do ; drawing

the rations ; serving out the rum, for each soldier
drinks it, or ought to do so, at the tub where it is
mixed and served ; if otherwise, individuals would
sell or give away their portion, and drunkenness
would be common. Providing tubs for this ; pre-
venting waste of water ; procuring wooden staves or
sticks for sentries, for arms are dangerous when many
regiments are mixed up on board ship, and frays are
likely to occur—these are a few absolute requirements
demanding prompt attention.

But just as a party fight commenced between
two rival corps, the general came to pay a final visit
of inspection. Lithe in figure and active in movement, in the prime of life, he quickly gained the
deck. All eyes were fixed on him, and forthwith a
parade was ordered.

Now in a vessel made to carry about six hundred
passengers, it is impossible to muster nine hundred
men on deck. However, a third was got together,
to whom the general addressed a few words. He
said "their country watched them—that he ardently
wished he could be with them—that in heart he would
be—that life on board ship was delightful, and he
had found it so ;" then jumping from the seat on

which he was standing, he descended the side of the vessel, and was gone.

The speech put the men in good humour, and brought a smile on the cheeks of many a half sea-sick recruit at the idea of happiness on board ship. Many have since found there was not only happiness but luxury, too, compared with the tedium and constant labour of working parties in the trenches.

How carefully every word addressed by a commander to troops should be considered. Each sentence is subsequently canvassed, each syllable weighed. For whatever may be the understanding or intellect of the individual soldier it is certain that, in ordinary matters, the aggregate intellect of the number of men composing a company, a detachment, or regiment as a whole, forms usually a most just conclusion, and has the clearest notion of character. It would seem as if the particles of the good sense of the majority combined ; but be this as it may, the judgment of the body is seldom wrong. For several days our ship was named the " Eden's Eden."

The voyage was not distinguished by much incident. The wonders of the deep ; the hopes of sighting land ; an occasional fight; a case of small-pox; steps for pre-

vention of infection ; the ship's steward selling liquor
to the soldiers ; the captain's anger ; a sail in sight ;
a passing steamer homeward bound and conversation
by signal flags formed the only variation.

The fourth day brought us off the Rock of Lisbon ;
the fifth saw us steaming rapidly through the Straits
of Gibraltar. The captain keeping mid-channel, the
distance and haze prevented our having a good view
of the scene of former British gallantry, Tarifa.
The Rock of Gibraltar itself, so fondly remembered
by many of those on board who had been formerly
quartered there, merely loomed out of the mist and
scarcely allowed more than its huge outline to be
seen.

Three days more and, with glorious weather peculiar to the Mediterranean, we were steaming merrily
along between Sicily and the rocky island of Pan-
tellarea, and the same night anchored at Malta.
Described by many a traveller, it is unnecessary to
say more than, Eastern in aspect, Moorish in archi-
tecture, with flat-roofed houses, and European com-
forts, Malta is a link between Europe and Africa.
By arbitrary settlement it is appropriated to the
former quarter of the world; but rightly, from

climate, aspect, and inhabitants it ought to be reckoned as African.

To those who have never seen an Eastern town Malta will convey a fair but too favourable notion of one. The Italian and French languages, or a jargon of both, interspersed with English, are commonly spoken—in most of the respectable shops English is common, but a patois of Arabic is the language of the lowest class.

The fortifications, the governor's palace—formerly the residence of the Grand Master of the Knights of Malta—the pictures there, the Church of St. John, with the whole of its mosaic floor, forming monuments to the different knights buried therein, each emblazoned with the arms of the deceased; the Florian parade and barracks, the quarantine harbour, and the naval hospital are only a few of the objects a visitor to Malta should attentively inspect.

Having taken in fresh water, disembarked a few who were already invalids, and made additions to our already too numerous party, we left the beautiful harbour as usual amidst the unmeaning cheers from shore and ship, the garrisons of St. Elmo and Fort Antorius being the principal actors.

B

Passing in the course of a few days Cape Matapan, running through the intricate navigation of the Zea and Doro channels, we sighted Tenedos and Lemnos, and entered the Dardanelles. Steaming between the forts we lay to off the British Consul's at the village of Dardanelles, held a conversation by signals for an hour, and then proceeded.

To the north on the European shore the hills and country where the allied armies had been encamped near the village of Gallipoli were plainly visible. As for the scenery there is nothing very beautiful in passing the Dardanelles. Strange objects, however, appear:—the camels grazing, the costumes of the inhabitants, the build of the houses, the singular forts, the uncouth boats, the cultivation and apparent fertility, the distant hills, a stray tent here and there, the Turkish flag, all mostly seen through the telescope strangely impressing those who have for the first time left their native land with the realities of the east, exceeding in strangeness and variety every preconceived idea derived from books ; the sky, too, without a cloud, and the climate just warm enough to enjoy the evening breeze ;—the whole producing new thoughts, hopes, and emotions.

Having diminished our speed, steaming slowly as night closed in, we entered the Sea of Marmora ; as daylight broke the following morning most of us were on deck to catch the first view of Constantinople. But what a contrast in the weather had a few short hours produced! A bitterly cold northeaster prevailed as we caught sight of the hospital of Scutari on the Asiatic side, rising out of a bank of fog hanging over the shore. It was that torpid sort of dense heavy mist which prevails in these localities, with fever as the sure accompaniment, and where, as the sun sets, the miasma steams up and continues until dispersed by the next morning's heat. In tropical climates such localities are, if possible, avoided.

The distant slabs standing about the hospital showed the resting-place of many a British officer. How thickly sown these melancholy tributes appeared! And yet they were not a tithe of the numbers since erected there. On the European shores tall buildings, like manufactories, edged the coast, approaching the mosques and minarets of Constantinople. Perhaps the want of sun, or the bitter wind and chilly atmosphere, or possibly too highly wrought anticipations caused disappointment. The

view did not equal our expectations. It was only
when rounding the Seraglio Point that the grandeur
of the scene burst upon us. The Mosque of St
Sophia and the Seraglio first draw the attention, but
hardly can enquiries be made before the vessel, steaming on, brings to the view numerous minarets, the
palaces lining the European shore, the magnificent
bay or inlet termed the Golden Horn, dividing
Stamboul from Pera and Galata. The succession of
houses, domes, and public buildings covering the
whole side of the hill, interspersed here and there
with gardens, rivet the gaze, and fill the mind with
admiration and delight.

No sooner is the anchor dropped than numerous
caïques assemble round the ship, some filled with
small articles of merchandise such as looking glasses,
otto of roses, oranges, pipes, and tobacco ; the vendors
and boatmen, dressed in a loose sort of shirt of the
thinnest texture, with breeches like bags (formed most
conveniently for the punishment said to be sometimes
inflicted by pashas, namely, ordering a cat to be
placed in a culprit's nether garments), gabbling unknown tongues, with a word or two of English or
French interspersed, endeavour to vend their wares,

whilst others supplicate for hire.   " Tophana ! hey ! hey ! " " You come Tophana, Englis ! " " No buey no caïque, Johnny ! "   " Here good ! "   Squabbling and fighting amongst themselves to gain access to the side of the ship, these and similar ejaculations formed no very pleasant sounds—but the scene was amusing in the extreme.

Preferring an English boat to the caïque we were landed at the Tophana, or Ordnance Wharf, our uniform procuring for us entrance to the arsenal.   A ragged Turkish sentry called his superior, who was not a much more respectable individual.   Then began our first efforts to communicate by signs, but the offices of the admiral and port were not to be so discovered.   At length spying a Frenchman, we hailed him, and he, with the inherent civility of his country, becoming our temporary interpreter, and conducted by a Turkish soldier—one of the guards—we sallied forth up one of the narrowest, steepest, stoniest of hills, slippery with the vilest mud, with occasional holes suited for traps for the unwary, for those who, like ourselves, were strangers in Constantinople, until we reached the Hotel de l'Europe, close to the Post Office.

With what pleasure did we see there the rough

faces and garb of two or three British soldiers!
Abandoning our Turkish guide with a backsheesh,
which did not content him, we endeavoured to ascertain from them the required localities.

It was part of our duty to visit the admiral.   His
office seemed a chaos of sounds.   Orders and counter
orders were being given :—water ordered for one
ship, coals for another, in the midst of enquiries as to
arrivals and departures, and of news from the
east.

We were shortly afterwards ushered into the admiral's presence, and received with kindness and ur-
banity we little expected, judging from the glimpse we
had had of his treatment of his subordinate officials.
But he was all bustle, and after learning that fuel and
water were nearly sufficient, we were ordered off the
same afternoon.

Entering the boat in which the letters for Scutari
were conveyed, we determined to visit the hospital.
A scramble at landing, and we were at once amongst
Turkish boatmen, invalid and convalescent soldiers
going to and from the hospital, idlers on the wharf,
vendors and military purchasers of cabobs, vegetables,
and fish, but pushing our way at last we mounted the

hill leading to the immense pile forming the hospital. The apartments at the entrance were occupied by the recently appointed brigadier, Lord William Paulet. It was the head quarters of the commandant, yet, at no great distance from the gate, a dog and a bullock were lying dead, and an orderly (who turned out to be drunk) asleep beside them. A crowd of convalescents near the door led us to inquire of a man belonging to our own corps for some of our sick and wounded, but whilst professing to know them he was utterly ignorant. An assertion made at one moment was contradicted the next. Such a one had been seen within a few days at a particular locality of this extensive building ; another, it was surmised, was dead. So and so was stated to be on guard. Hardly spoken before the information was contradicted, and the man was said to have embarked for England. Nothing definite could be ascertained.

No special part of the hospital was appropriated to any one division of the army, much less to a brigade, or to a regiment. Consequently it was utterly vain, during our short stay, to see the sick inmates belonging to our own corps. They were inextricably intermixed, and to have found even a few it would have been necessary to search every part, and go throughout this huge hospital.

Lord William Paulet, who had just then assumed command, very quickly remedied the disorder, and assisted by an efficient but too small staff instilled vigour and method into the arrangements; but for this his successor was destined to reap the benefit and credit, to be applauded, and finally, to his own great surprise, to be decorated by our Most Gracious Queen with the Knight Commander's decoration of the Honourable Order of the Bath, hitherto believed to be the reward of those only who had commanded in action.

Bidding farewell to this seat of disease and misery (which we all sincerely prayed it might never be the fortune of war for us to inhabit as patients), we embarked in a caïque for our transport.

Novel as this sort of boat appears on the water, still more so is it to a passenger, and it requires considerable experience to get in and out with safety. The living freight sits down in the bottom of the stern on a cushion, with the head raised just sufficiently to be able to see over its side. He then reclines, and nothing should induce him to stand up.

Luxuriously reposing, the rowers, with a long steady stroke, bear him speedily along, gliding imperceptibly and swiftly through the water.   The motion resembles that of a canoe.   Passing the Ladies' Tower, a small rock on the Asiatic side to which a romantic story is attached, we were soon on board our ship, the anchor was weighed, and we bade adieu, a final adieu, alas ! for many of us, to Constantinople, and its opposite neighbour, Scutari.

CHAPTER II.

NOTHING can be more lovely or enchanting than the views on each side in passing through the Bosphorus, the hills and mountains trending down in some places to the very water's edge ; in others abruptly disclosing bays and creeks. Both banks are thickly studded with houses, but the European side may be said to be one continuous town reaching from Constantinople to Buykudere, and where the Turkish contingent was subsequently organised and stationed. The dwellings of the Turks on the Asiatic side seemed to possess every comfort suited to a summer residence, and large baths or bathing rooms allowing a free current of water could be observed attached to many dwellings.

Here and there on the tops of the hills old towers

and ruins appeared, to most of which some classic
romance or tale is attached. The foliage above and
down to the water, interspersed with cypress groves
marking the resting-place of former dwellers on the
lovely· shore, enrich the landscape ; and the small
passenger steam boats running frequently between
Therapia, Buykudere, and Constantinople, filled with
people—Turks, Christians, and Jews—offer strange
pictures to the stranger.

Darkness closed in whilst we were much enjoying
these scenes ; as we entered the Black Sea on the
following afternoon the high iron-bound coast of the
Crimea was just visible. In the evening we dropped
anchor in Balaclava Bay, after a voyage of little more
than twenty-eight hours from Constantinople. We
fired a gun, and signalled with rockets and blue lights,
but no notice was taken of us from the shore.

In the morning, however, the signal station began
to work, and the captain was ordered to report himself. Balaclava Bay presents a grand appearance.
High cliffs and detached rocks form its coast, and, in
a southerly wind, threaten destruction to any unfortunate ship that drags or breaks from her anchorage,
affording to the passengers and sailors a poor chance

for life, for the sea then dashes in with such violence
that, even if escape from the waves could be hoped
for, the rocky shore allows no footing.

A wall running down from the signal tower along
the side of the hill terminating in a point of land,
and the topmasts of a ship or two visible above it,
show where the harbour is to be found; but the
entrance cannot be seen, and is only discovered on
rounding the point, which, from the anchorage in
the bay, seems merely to form part of the coast. As
you enter it is on the right, and, bending to the
westward, is called " Castle Point," whilst on the right
it is designated " Cossack Point."

The harbour itself at its entrance is not more than
fifty yards wide, and no part is a third of the width
of the Thames at London Bridge. Many a ship
might sail or steam past it without even guessing
there was a secure haven; it brings to recollection
the description given in Dampier's " History of the
Buccaneers," of their favourite refuges in the New
World; and in former ages, Balaclava harbour might
well have been the resort of pirates. The town, or
rather village, is at the foot of two long ranges of
hills averaging about six hundred feet in height.

Accompanying the captain, with some difficulty
we found a suitable landing place, as the harbour
was choked with shipping. An elderly gentleman
in the garb of a naval officer, busily pulling about
the harbour in his gig, observed and put us ashore,
his kindly act belying the reputation he had unfortunately acquired for roughness and incivility. It was
the late Admiral Boxer, one of the many now no more.

The so-called Ordnance Wharf, if a few boards
sunk on the shore deserve the name, was the spot
where we first landed at Balaclava. Wading through
mud (for it had been wet weather), in no place less
than six inches deep, in many much more, we reached
the hospitable quarters of the Assistant Quarter-
Master General, Major Mackenzie.

A few wooden steps rising about eight feet from
the ground, brought us to a sort of dilapidated
verandah, under which was the door of one of the
best houses in Balaclava. The walls were thick, and
of course there were windows. A fire-place, or what
supplied the place of one, inserted in the angle of the
wall, was shown with no small pride as the result of
superior handicraft. The yard below was filled with
animals of all sorts, and with every description

of covering—sorry nags ; half-starved " bâts " * carefully covered up ; others without blankets, and
fastened by the bridle but without saddle ; others
with saddle, but a rope in place of the bridle ;
servants working and preparing breakfast, raised on
a sort of bank a few inches above the mud so as to
form an impediment to the loss or running off of the
manure, and such as is often seen in a farmyard.

Having finished our business it was no easy
matter to return. The lanes were intricate to a new-
comer, and such lanes as they were at that time it is
difficult to describe, yet they were in a better condition than they had been. There were French and
English, crowds of animals, drivers of all nations,
artillery waggons, fatigue parties, mules with warm
clothing, bats with forage and comestibles struggling
together, pushing on to or returning from their respective goals, but plunging on, and making constant
enquiries, we endeavoured to retrace our steps.

Asking the route of one of that gallant amphibious
corps the marines, he pointed to a passage about a
yard in width, with loose rocks on both sides—apparently a gutter made to conduct the mud and water

* Pack horses.

from the hillside to the sea. Seeing us hesitate and look around for another path, this good-natured fellow (for so he ought to be considered, when many vouchsafed no answer either by voice or gesture), observed, " Never fear, there is good bottom ; " and so, probing our way with a stick, we found, under twelve or eighteen inches of the most villanous mud and stones of every size, a solid foundation. This passage led to the water's edge, but there our difficulties greatly increased : the boats were there, but the boatmen refused to take us. No offer of money produced any effect, and when the crews heard we wished to proceed to a vessel in the bay—with a stiff breeze blowing—they laughed incredulously, as if we were attempting to foist a bad joke upon them.

Wandering for two or three hours in search of a boat, but without success, we eventually sought refuge on board a transport, full of sick, bound for Constantinople; and at last, through the kindness of a naval commander in one of the Queen's steam-tugs, we were despatched to our ship.

The variety of costume at Balaclava far exceeded that in more civilised climes, and " classes " were scarcely to be distinguished ; officers and soldiers

alike had—the fortunate ones—boots and leggings,
trousers according to fancy, sheepskin coats or jackets,
—the latter made as if some economical contractor
had designedly cut off the coat tails in order to put
money in his pocket, regardless of the disfigurement
and discomfort of the wearers ; a ragged red coattee
skin skull-cap, with the hair outwards.

Then again there were French troops, dirty it is
true, and with worn garments, but in precisely the
same costume in which they may be seen in Stras-
bourg or Paris.

The newly-arrived English soldiers were instantly
recognised ; there was with them some remains of
dress and attempts occasionally at a military salute.
What were once neat soldiers of the 11th Hussars
could now only be identified as such by a glimpse of
the cherry-coloured pantaloons peeping out between
the haybands wound round the leg as far as the knee,
and the economically cut sheepskin coat.   They were
mounted on animals which, in England, would have
subjected the riders to an indictment under Martin's
Act.

It was whilst looking at these wondrous sights
that two young boys, officers evidently fresh from

England and just down from the front, as the plateau where the troops engaged in the siege were encamped was called, rushed up with the query, "Can you tell us where Mr Russell lives?" Being unable and idle, we watched their movements, and thus learned the abode of the *Times'* correspondent. It was of stone, in very wretched repair, in such a condition as at home would have drawn a string of complaints from· the peasant doomed to inhabit it. There was a small yard in front where several horses were tied up, showing that their riders were inside, refreshing themselves or imparting information, or perhaps combining both duties; victuals and drink in exchange for matter to amuse or to enlighten the British public.

A short time afterwards we were introduced to this literary celebrity. His appearance has been often described. He is stout, about five feet eleven inches in height, round face, black hair and whiskers, a pair of excessively bright intelligent dark eyes, dressed at that time like a sportsman, wearing a cap with a gold band. Agreeable in manner, witty in conversation, a jovial companion, an addition to a camp dinner, Mr Russell seldom fails to make a friend when oppor-

c

tunity offers, or to meet a hearty welcome amongst his legion of military acquaintances.

The wind freshening we were ordered by signal to weigh and rendezvous at Cape Chersoncse. Steaming along to the westward, we passed the Monastery of St George, with its terraced garden extending down a third of the cliff, thence continued by trees descending nearly to the beach. A short distance further on after passing this conspicuous object; the coast slopes gradually down until it descends almost to the level of the sea, and ending in a low spit of sand on the farthest point of which stands the lighthouse. From the sea across this spit vessels could be seen safely riding at anchor, whilst on the shore the French tents stretching far into the distance and the soldiers on parade were visible.

Rounding the lighthouse, after some signalling with Sir Edmund Lyon's ship, we cast anchor in smooth water. Then it was we caught our first view of Sebastopol, with Fort Constantine on the north side, the Quarantine on the south, the Russian flag floating from what we surmised was the Telegraph Battery, with the top-masts of the sunken vessels of the enemy just visible.

The French approaches and their tents covered the
ground to the south-west of the town, and the allied
ships on guard, scattered like dots seaward, at a
respectful distance from the Russian forts and harbour, but still showing the enemy how carefully they
were watched, and how hazardous would be any
attempt to evade the blockade, was a sight which
caused each heart to beat with hope, and made us
congratulate ourselves on the good fortune which had
driven us to Kazatch Bay, giving us an opportunity
of seeing more of Sebastopol and its harbour than
many who had been out during the whole campaign.

The loud roaring of guns, too, told plainly that
this glorious sight was no pleasure scene, that it was
no experimental summer rendezvous, that it was no
review of the fleet, but that all was real,—we were
in the presence of actual strife, and navy and army
were combined in deadly warfare against no unworthy
antagonist.

Notwithstanding the weather, instead of resting
many of us that night paced the deck watching the
flashing of the guns, listening to the sound, and
speculating on the distance. Full of confident hope,
many dreamed of despatches, honours, and distinc-

tions ; whilst many others,—alas ! now no more, snapped off in the flower of youth, health, and strength,—dwelt on that fate to which they were shortly to be called.

After about thirty-six hours' stay off Kamiesch, we were ordered back to Balaclava, where, on arrival, we were provokingly ordered to stand out to sea. But as all pain and pleasure must have an end, so did our contre-temps; on returning in the morning we joyfully hailed the signal, " Prepare to come into harbour," and that very day, after hauling and pulling, stopping, and steaming round the Castle Point, and making way through the over-crowded harbour, we securely moored close to the Ordnance Wharf.

The town now presented a more agreeable appearance than on our former visit. The weather had been dry with a very strong breeze, and positively the mud was not more than eight inches deep,—in some parts the road was dry. But the lessened depth of mud was no real advantage : what it lost in watery particles and depth was counterbalanced by its glutinous solidity. To get rid of it now required actual scrubbing and scraping, whereas before only washing was necessary.

Boats being provided, each detachment with its
camp equipment was landed successively at the head
of the harbour, until the whole of the troops were
disembarked. Then marching about three-quarters
of a mile we began to ascend, and encamped on the
. slope of a hill or mountain running down until it
reached the level on the west side of the road between Kadikoi and Balaclava.

This must not be pictured as a nice, smooth, glassy
slope. Rocks abounded, rills of water percolated
and issued down amongst the natural and artificial
drains, and two ravines so steep as to oblige those
desirous of going from one division to the other (for
the drafts belonging to the several regiments were
placed together according to the divisions to which
their corps belonged and they were destined to join)
intersected our encampment, and forced them to
proceed round their base. In one part was a regiment
about three weeks landed, on our right some Croats
were encamped ; across the road and valley lay the
remnant of the Turks. This valley was a desolate
looking extent of flooded land, ditches, banks, and
burying grounds, where, only four months before, a
luxuriant orchard and vineyard had flourished. Far

away in the distance on the slope of the hill stood
the church or chapel of Kamara, and upon close
observation stray Cossacks (part of the Cossack
picket), might be seen watching the English proceedings.

‑ Fortunately officers and men were each provided
with a day's cooked provisions, for, after the tents
were pitched, holes and fire-places had to be constructed : although a dry ditch favoured us, slow progress was made in this direction. Like the rest of
the troops our recruits had to take their first lesson
in misery immediately on arrival, from their ignorance and inability to cook, but going to the encampment in their front, they profited by example, and
soon completed cooking pits.

As a matter of course, some pits were pronounced
faultless, whilst others could not be made to answer
their purpose, but necessity is a stern master and a
more effectual teacher than Cobham or Aldershot.
That which is once learned by the first is seldom forgotten, whilst the knowledge acquired at the experimental camps, being only partial (cooking houses of
solid brick having been in some instances constructed
by artisans) is not of the essential utility contem-

plated and desired, so far as tuition is concerned, nor
does it afford any ultimate practical advantage.

Perhaps the lesson "from necessity" could not
well be inculcated at home. The cry of "cruelty"
and "harsh treatment" would be raised, and the
experience that might thus be gained and utilised is
lost.

Independently of cooking other difficulties arose.
Every atom of food, such as bread, rice, sugar, rum,
barrels of pork or beef, etc., had to be brought from
Balaclava by the manual labour of the consumers.
The officers of the commissariat, not satisfied with the
recorded numerical strength of the regiments, insisted
on being furnished with accurate and elaborate calculations of the number of pounds, ounces, and fractions
of ounces required,—if this were not done, articles
were refused and the return sent back for correction by
these gentlemen,—proverbially careful of themselves,
but utterly regardless of the useless expenditure of
labour, and the craving empty stomachs of the men.

It so happened that one of our first nights in the
trenches was that bitter one in the month of February,
when Sir Colin Campbell's proposed reconnaissance
failed, owing to the severity of the weather. The

evening set in with a slight drizzle with the wind from the southwest. Later on its violence increased, and it blew stiff enough to make us tremble for our tent poles. Towards eleven o'clock the frost set in, and snow of the finest quality rapidly fell. Never, either in America or elsewhere, had such fine grained snow been seen. There was no escape, every crevice of our tents was penetrated, bed-covering, boots, and even the mattress received a portion, and by the aid of the frost our blankets became like hard useless boards.

How devoutly did we wish for day-light! and when the day at last broke, we then first learned that an expedition had been out in such a pitiless night. By the help of a small tea-kettle heated with naphtha, our party obtained about three table spoonsful of tea. "Tea without milk or sugar," some will exclaim, "how nauseous!" "How disagreeable," will the luxurious exclaim. It was neither, but on the contrary was the most grateful restorative, and we voted the " Ætna" worth its weight in gold.

After such a night, having calculated pounds and ounces for our friends of the commissariat, it was no easy matter to write them with the ink frozen, or

when, after carefully holding the bottle between the
legs or next the body to thaw the liquid, to find
a moment's exposure blasted, or rather, froze our
hopes, and we saw that the only result of a pen on
paper was to scatter gritty particles in vain efforts
to write figures. Reflection and the Ætna solved
the difficulty, and the labour was at length completed.

Speculatingly we watched Sir Colin's columns. In
the heavy snow they were lost sight of, then seen
again, and later in the day it became certain the
troops were returning. Various reports were current,
but it was not till some weeks later the English newspapers gave something like a correct version.

Our sojourn between Kadikoi and Balaclava was
not destined to be prolonged. After General Estcourt
(the lamented Adjutant-General), had looked at us,
the detachments were gradually moved off, and within
eight days from our landing all had joined their
respective regiments.

During our stay heavy firing went on nightly at
the front, which we plainly heard ; although seven
miles distant, it was singular, whilst lying in our tent
so far from the scene, the flashes, apparently of light-

ning, were distinctly visible, but, if the wind happened to set towards Balaclava, the reports which followed left no doubt of their origin.

These heavy firings at night caused much conversation—sometimes we heard the English had been attacked, then it was the French. Stories from the front increased in dimensions the more distant they were from their origin.

It was after such a very heavy fire which surprised even those comparatively old soldiers encamped in our vicinity, that we determined to go to the front and pay a visit to our own division ; we set out, notwithstanding the weather, or rather the state of the ground, for the genial sun daily turned into glutinous mud the results of the night's frost, only to be turned again to a composition resembling adamant by the next morning.

Crossing the hill on which we were encamped, and descending close to the cavalry camp a little above the village of Kadikoi, we endeavoured to find the quarters of a field officer of heavy dragoons. After various enquiries, and being sent from encampment to encampment, we reached the camp of the Enniskillens, where, in answer to our question, a sergeant with a rich Irish brogue said, "Shure, there is the mayjer himself, with the red shirt, feeding the thurkeys." And there, truly, was visible the upper part of our friend's body leaning out of a sunken tent, in the very act described, and a goodly number of poultry had evidently repaid his care.

At the worst of times the troops encamped close to Balaclava and Kadikoi had the advantage of being able to procure their rations and the officers' delicacies, without the excessive labour which those in the front underwent.

Returning again towards the latter village, crossing the gorge near Sir Colin Campbell's quarters, and following a foot-track, we plunged through a water course half-filled with snow, not without sundry misgivings, and commenced the gradual ascent of the slope to the plateau on which Turks, French, and English were encamped.

Bleak indeed was the prospect. The track was so deep in mud as to cover the horses' legs up to the knees at each step, and it was only by great care, patience, and attention we avoided accidents. Lying about here and there were the remains of horses which had sunk famished and exhausted under their burthens ; and struggling parties of men going to and coming from Balaclava were occasionally met.

Turning off to the right from the beaten track, and following the rough line of defence, we ascended a somewhat steep cliff, and on surmounting it found ourselves in the Turkish camp. Tracking the route by the marks of straggling troops, passing the French encampment (part of Bosquet's division), we reached the celebrated Woronzoff Road.

From this point the view was grand in the extreme. The whole of the plateau, as far as the eye could reach, was covered with canvas. A few huts showed the position of the British light division, and the great landmark for strangers, indeed, the delightful goal for the fatigued and heavy laden returning home, the grim " windmill " was seen beyond.

CHAPTER III.

It was at the point where the track to Balaclava
intersects the Woronzoff Road we now saw one of the
dread realities of war—wounded men. On the previous night there had been a sharp attack by the
French against the fort or outwork (subsequently
taken on the 7th June), known as the White Buildings. The French, for the moment successful, were
roughly handled, and eventually obliged to retire.
It was rumoured that this was caused by a battalion
of their marines having gone to the right about
without orders—in other words, had precipitately fled.

The loss was heavy. Strings of mules, bearing
a cariole on both sides containing its unfortunate burden, proved that the number of wounded was not
slight. Some were sitting, others recumbent. The
most ghastly were those hurt in the face or head, the
bandages concealing the nature of the wound, and
the gore, oozing out, led the imagination to picture a
worse hurt than perhaps had actually been sustained.

The cariole itself is an iron framework made somewhat in the form of two large steps, but somewhat
like easy or portable arm chairs, having hinges at the
angles. Should the patient be able to sit up, the
platform or step for the feet, of the same size as the
seat, is let down ; but if the contrary, the canvas
covered iron framework is straitened at the hinges,
the back of the chair is lowered to a convenient
angle, the part intended for the feet raised, the canvas
loosened, the arms raised, and the wounded man is
enabled to recline in a rough, but far from uneasy
litter.

Very different is this from the sort of hearse ambulance supplied to the English, suggested to the Secretary at War by, and made under the superintendence
of, an officer better known by reputation for his pub-

lications relating to army statistics than for any military experience, gained in actual warfare or even
such as may be acquired on colonial service.

These ambulances were made without springs, or
with springs so rough as to cause motion quite sufficient in itself to bruise and injuriously shake a sound
man,—God help a wounded one ! Hearses would
have been a more appropriate name for these vehicles,
which opened in the rear, the back being let down like
the door of the hind boot of a coach. Inside were two
compartments, a lower and an upper, a firm division
dividing them lengthways. A sliding framework of
wood, covered with canvas, is drawn out and placed
on the ground, into which the sufferer is lifted, the
frame raised and slid, with its mutilated or sick living
contents, into the vehicle, somewhat in the manner a
pianoforte is carted by Messrs Broadwood, and with
much less care than a coffin is usually put into a
hearse.

A similar process occurs with the upper berth.
Here two more patients are slid in on the near side,
the back of the boot is fastened and locked up, and
away starts the ambulance, jolting and rattling over
hill and dale, the sufferers inside laying their faces

close to the gratings or holes at each side to obtain
a little air, at the mercy of the driver on the box, who
could not catch the loudest cry from the sufferers on
account of the noise of the vehicle as it travels along.

Turning to the left down the Woronzoff Road, proceeding through the lines of the second brigade of
the light division, we arrived at the tent of a friend.
Scarcely a year had elapsed since we had shaken the
hands, which were shortly afterwards laid low. The
gallant officer's care-worn face now showed that hardships, mental anxiety for his men, and a somewhat
fretful temper had done their work ;—the soldier of
forty-five looked like a civilian nearly sixty years of
age.

A hearty welcome greeted his former subaltern,
and a substantial repast of ham, brackish water, and
sherry satisfied the not very fastidious taste of his
guest. The provisions were laid out on a piece of
board, making an excellent table, and shown as a
good specimen of the handicraft of one of the men.
Stores of tea were lying about the marquee, and a
bell tent immediately in rear, full of all sorts of com-
forts sent gratuitously from England for the soldiers,
evidenced that, at any rate, the resources for the corps

were now plentiful, and were carefully husbanded. A short "farewell," and we returned to our camp between Kadikoi and Balaclava.

Sunday in camp is an impressive scene notwithstanding that the duties, laborious works, and fatigue parties are detailed and carried on as during weekdays. The service is performed in hollow squares—a human wall surrounding the clergyman, under a nobler roof than ever could be made by human hands, the canopy of heaven, and so forming the temple. Its brevity and simplicity carry religion to the very soul, rivet attention, and bring the mind, too often wandering on such occasions, to the very theme, to the very pith of the subject.

This is the feeling on ordinary occasions. But change the scene, and let it be laid in front of a brigade forming part of a division at the front. Then the solemn booming of the guns, the distractions of the moment, the excitement caused by the bursting of a shell or shells, and the knowledge that fierce and deadly war is the cause of our being on the spot, bring to the mind the uncertainty of life, and often make the heart give extra throbs as the thought of the narrow escapes of the week in discharging the

D

duties of the trenches passed rapidly before the
mind.

Is this gratitude ? Is it weakness ? Is it the
feeling that, through some hidden merit of our own,
we have been spared ? Whatever the feeling may be
there is no denying that, on these sacred, solemn
occasions it pervaded most breasts, and that, scarcely
anywhere in the world could be seen a more devout,
sincere, and contrite congregation than was presented
by the officers assembled in that humble deal hut on
the Sunday morning to partake of the Lord's Supper.

The party to which we belonged, with glad feelings, now left our Balaclava encampment to proceed
to that which was termed " The Front ; " in a word,
to join our regiments, and participate in the siege.

The critical moment was near at hand. For months
casual shots only had been exchanged ; there had been
no real firing from the English lines. We were slowly
carrying on and proceeding with our approaches, and
since the early part of December there had been no
attempt to hinder us. The Russians were making
their own defences, or more properly, were engaged
skilfully and silently in effecting approaches, actually
hemming in the besiegers. And there can be no doubt,

whilst the Russians held the line of the Tchernaya, the allied forces were as much besieged by the Russians as the Russians were in Sebastopol. In a word, the enemy, having continued to hold the White Buildings against the attacks of the French, were gradually forming works up to, and on, and pushing forward approaches from the Mamelon Verte. A few small holes first appeared, with stones or insignificant walls in front of them. These suddenly, generally after a quiet night, became more numerous ; they were then connected, a line of defence established, earth-works thrown up, a battery formed, and at last the apex of this became known as " the Mamelon Verte," or what, to the British mind may be a better term, for both denominations were equally common, " Gordon's Hill."

Honour and praise to the excellent engineer Gordon who had charge of the right attack. It was said in camp, and it was the conversation of the Light Division, that Gordon, on the first arrival of the army before Sebastopol, pointed out the east side as the proper point of attack. It was reported that he declared the Malakoff to be the key of the position, and advised that our approaches should commence from the Mamelon Verte—thus this important hillock obtained the designation of " Gordon's Hill."

It is well known that for many months the Mamelon was uncared for by the allies. Whether Gordon's plans would have required a larger covering army than was in the power of the allies to give, with due regard to their left, and to the enemy, who shortly afterwards occupied the line of the Tchernaya, matters little now. Some cogent reason unquestionably must have existed for breaking ground at a different point.

And the eyes of the allies were only really opened to the mistake which had been made when they found the enemy had established the Mamelon as its advanced work, had connected it with the Malakoff, had thrown up lines of approach in front of the left face of the Great Redan, had then connected these three several works, shortly afterwards making further advances, and thus actually, though designated the besieged, in a measure were also the besiegers.

It was a few days prior to the 11th March 1855, that the intention of the enemy to seize the Mamelon became obvious. At that moment the 2d division of the English army, under the gallant Pennefather, still occupied their encampment on the Inkerman side of the plateau. The French were in considerable force in rear of the light division, shortly afterwards much increasing their strength, our ally taking up the whole lines of attack in front and to the right of the same division. Thus the British works on the right were about to be connected with the French left nearly in front of the middle ravine.

This ravine was common to both the English and French, the former having formed a covered way on the left up to the 21-gun or Gordon's battery, whilst the latter went direct into their works. This English covered way was made with vast labour, in many parts hewn out of solid rock, or by blowing it out with gunpowder. The necessity for the covered way was forced on the scientific branch of the service, the Royal Engineers, after the trenches had been opened, and valuable lives sacrificed in crossing the spaces between the camp and the works.

The British right attack may thus be said to have been bounded on its right by the middle ravine, and on its left by the Woronzoff road, which there wound down into the town through precipitous land, the right bank being the termination of that which was

denominated the right attack, whilst the left side was
the right of the British left attack : thus the British
were connected at the Woronzoff road, and the ex-
tremes of each were joined with the French.

The lines of our ally were very different from those
of the British. They were most solid and regular : a
perfect study. Six or seven banquettes one above the
other inside, like steps, permitted numerous defenders
of all sizes and heights to be securely located, to work
effectually, and to deliver their fire in natural positions. But with us, alas! in wet weather to stand at
all on the single, sloping, slippery broken banquettes
was no easy task, and to fire was, in many places,
impossible.

It was after a period of some months' silence, when
the enemy's proceedings at the Mamelon Verte became palpable, that Lord Raglan determined on the
11th of March to endeavour to prevent the activity
of the Russian troops. A certain number of rounds
from the 21-gun battery was ordered to be fired. It
was an afternoon's interesting study through our sand-
bag loopholes to watch the effect. Shot and shell
were both fired, many of the latter with excessive
want of precision, bursting anywhere but at the place

intended, owing to the antiquity of the fuses. Nor were the Russians idle,—no sooner did we attempt to annoy their working parties than they fell to also, from guns at the Redan and in front of the Malakoff. For every British shot at least four Russian were returned, as if the enemy wished to prove that, at any rate, ammunition was plentiful.

The sight was interesting. Whenever the British shot or shell went close, or seemed threatening, the Russians at the Mamelon would run off the work, and, separating into small bodies, in parties of, perhaps, a dozen or less, would get behind the heaps of stones which had first formed the ambuscade or rifle-pit. In cover of this description it was useless wasting the fire of heavy guns, and accordingly, after a couple of hours, the cannonading ceased about six in the evening.

It may not be unimportant to state that, in the beginning of March the guard in the trenches was on, nominally, for only twelve hours, but in reality it was nearly eighteen. This was rendered necessary because, as it was desirable to relieve the parties in the dark or dusk, the troops had to march from the camp at 3 A.M., and for a similar reason, to remain until it

became obscure, about 7 or 7.30 P.M. Those therefore
that went on duty in the evening had a short time,
but those in the day, a long and tedious watch.

On the evening of the 12th March a working party
of a thousand men was employed prolonging this
covered way to the right of what was termed " the
Old Advances," with a view to connect the British
with the French works in front of the Middle Ravine.
About the same time a mortar battery of 13-inch
heavy sea-service mortars was established on the spit
of ground in front of the 2d Brigade, Light Division,
about 100 yards in rear of the look-out post on
Frenchman's Hill, and on the left of the Middle
Ravine as we marched down to our works.

Great wonders were expected from those huge
mortars, but some fatality seemed connected with
them. Many shells burst in their flight, others again
were supposed to have gone completely over the
enemy's works into the harbour, and any effect produced was uncertain and rarely perceptible.

On the east side of the Ravine were many natural
caverns and caves, and just where it made a turn,
nearly at right angles, our allies the French established their ambulance, to which the wounded

were brought and attended in comparative security. Climbing up the bank about three quarters of a mile in front of the 1st Brigade, Light Division, stood the Victoria Redoubt, held by the French, a little in rear of their lines, and connecting the Middle Ravine with the Inkerman or White House Ravine.

From the Victoria Redoubt, which our allies were loth to let visitors enter, a very extensive view was obtained, showing almost the whole of the right attack and embracing the works of the Mamelon and Malakoff.

On the 13th of March Captain Craigie, of the Royal Engineers, was killed. He was returning cheerfully from his tour of duty and walking up a part of the Ravine usually considered to be out of fire, when a chance splinter from a shell struck him under the shoulder, reached his heart, and killed him on the spot.

Visiting some weeks afterwards the burial ground of right attack, the Royal Engineers, (which by that time had received the remains of several other officers from that gallant corps,) we saw a handsome stone had been placed over the grave of this lamented officer, inscribed, "To the Memory of a Captain, a

Comrade, and a Friend," erected by the non-commissioned officers and soldiers of his company, showing in brief but touching terms, the estimation in which he was held.

In the same row, and close together, also repose the remains of Bainbrigge, Crofton, King, Baynes, Greaves, Dawson (killed in his very first tour of duty in the trenches), Jesse, and some others, all of the Royal Engineers, belonging to the right attack.

It was expected there would be some very warm work on the evening of the 14th of March, and a heavy fire of musketry at seven, of about half-an-hour's duration, caused the Brigade to be ordered under arms. Thus we remained for some time, when we were sent home with orders to turn out again in half-an-hour. The time passed slowly, and just at the end of the half-hour, when we were hoping to get a little rest, we were again under arms. Thrice this operation took place that night, but without anything further happening.

The French, judging from the vague reports gathered in the morning, had been attacked by the Russians whilst prolonging their covered way towards the

English parallel, had repulsed the sortie, and then, advancing, had endeavoured to take the ambuscades or rifle-pits of the Russians, but in this attempt they were not successful.

The following night it was anticipated we should make good progress in connecting the French and British trenches. It was pitch dark, and highly advantageous for the undertaking. A covering party of three hundred men was detailed. "Covering parties" usually marched down in rear of the trench guard, and halted at a spot or rendezvous previously arranged. At this period of the siege a staff officer scarcely ever appeared to assist in the details or to carry out the orders.

The Guards' covering and working parties marched down to the rendezvous where the several commanders, captains, and subalterns, with small detachments from different regiments which were to form the party, led by the Engineers, were collected, and were placed under our command.

On this occasion, after moving off we were directed to halt at a particular locality, and there to wait for instructions before proceeding under the guidance of

an officer of the Engineers. It was deemed a somewhat critical duty, and our security as well as the
progress of the work depended much on not being
discovered. We were to cover the workers, who it
was confidently hoped would complete the junction
of the British trench with that of the French ; silence
was therefore indispensable.

Halted, we patiently waited the arrival of our
guide. Watching time passes tediously. Growing
impatient we began to fancy we had missed our
rendezvous, when the gigantic and mysterious figure
of Major Gordon, wrapped in a short cloak, appeared.
We say "mysterious figure," and so he was, for he
seemed ubiquitous in the trenches. At moments
least expected, at localities hardly dreamt of, this
energetic and gallant engineer rose up. His height
was about 6 feet 3 inches, his size in proportion, and
like a grim spectre, unexpected, he arrived.

Following him in single (or what perhaps is better
understood by saying Indian) file, we threaded what
even then seemed an interminable length of trench,
sometimes a foot deep only, sometimes in the open,
sometimes well sheltered, until at length we were
directed to extend our party, one-third sixty yards in

front of our line of operations, whilst the remainder
crouched down and lay close in that which was the
first commencement of a trench or cover.

The French, at no great distance from us, kept up
a continuous fire the whole night until day-break
and distracted the attention of the enemy, so that,
with the exception of a good many shells which fell
too close to be pleasant, we were fortunate.   All our
party was unhurt; the only noticeable incident
was when our gallant engineer was nearly shot
by one of our own sentries.   The line of sentries
having been extended, two detachments overlapped
and fired into each other, and thus endangered a
life more valuable than most to the army and the
country.

The scene of darkness, the marching down, the
passage in file through the works, the figure at the
head of the line remind one of those theatrical scenes
so often witnessed, so seldom actually realised.   In
many of our most important operations nothing could
prevail on our working parties to labour quietly; the
British soldier dislikes being debarred from the use
of his voice, or the enjoyment of his pipe; but in
this instance, though we heard the men at work, yet

it turned out, in the darkness, many had missed the
proper spot, or more likely had slunk away to sleep
until daylight, in the morning therefore only half the
number of yards of trench which ought to have been
executed was completed.

To such disappointments and trials are superintending officers of Engineers subject, for though
the men have a superabundance of courage they
have no disposition to labour : they imagine they did
not enlist for that. Wanting the ésprit or interest
which a French soldier frequently takes in the work
he is assisting to throw up, the Englishman requires
the constant watching, the persuasive representation of
his officers, the urging to labour which sometimes is
actually more essential and more his duty than the
mere sentry work and military routine to which he
may have been accustomed.

Nor is it merely in disposition to labour our men
were deficient.   There was an utter recklessness
about their arms.   Of course these were loaded, but
a rifle might be loaded for a week and no pains
taken by the owner to ensure the certainty of its
discharge when required, and on which his own life
might depend.   Accordingly, in most regiments, as

soon as the men came off the trenches they were
marched down to unload and discharge their arms,
and when properly cleaned to reload.

With the French on the other hand, each soldier,
after being relieved immediately looked to his arm,
and by the way discharged it as recklessly and as
regardless of the safety of those encamped around as
if they had been "Russians."

Saint Patrick's night, the 17th March 1855, was
one of excitement. The vicinity of our allies kept
us constantly on the qui vive ; whether there was
occasion or not there was generally a good deal of
noise in the way of musketry fire. On this night
the brigade was constantly under arms, and that not
needlessly, for the French were endeavouring to drive
out the enemy from the whole line of rifle pits. This
they succeeded in doing, but could not hold their
advantage ; the adversary sallied out in force from
the Mamelon, and not only reoccupied the pits, but,
entering the French works caused much confusion
and a considerable number of casualties.

Thus constant alarm was kept up, and at one time
the first brigade was moved down as if to act as a
support, whilst the second brigade of the Light

Division was marched to the front, towards our own works. Admitting that our gallant allies are patterns as soldiers, that their hand or wit can be modelled to meet any difficulty, it has been too much the fashion to decry the British and to condemn our men, yet in the quality of stubborn courage and bravery the English soldier is as superior by comparison to the French as the latter may be to the former when thrown upon their own resources, bearing in mind at the same time that, whilst one is taught to respect the rights of property, the others avowedly live by pillage.

In illustration of the quality of true courage it deserves to be noted, whilst in the British army it was invariably the custom during a fog at night, and on the approach of darkness, to throw out a line of sentries accompanied by their officers about forty or sixty yards in front of our works, the French never did so, and it was said that neither the discipline of their troops, nor the individual nerve of the men was sufficient to admit of their so doing; consequently in the French trenches, during the livelong night, there was constant pattering of musketry produced by their firing at stones, shadows, dogs, or any

other object which a lively imagination could conjure
into a Russian's grey-coat stealing along in the
darkness.

Saturdays and Sundays, being the usual periods of
the Russian reliefs and the arrival of reinforcements,
many of us were on the watch. Long trains of
mules could be seen wending their way on the north
side towards the water's edge, sometimes accompanied, at others preceded or followed by troops.
Thus it was on the 18th March, when a lengthy
column of men was seen, apparently waiting for
nightfall to be conveyed across to Sebastopol, and
estimated at above five thousand.

As before a storm of the elements unusual calm-
ness prevails, so, prior to a serious attack, sortie, or
encroachment of the enemy there generally occurred
remarkable stillness, with almost entire cessation from
firing. Such ominous quiet usually caused anxiety,
and rendered the French guard more watchful.

Tranquillity of this nature prevailed between the
19th and 21st of March. On the former day an
unfortunate accident (for so casualties were designated), happened in one of the regiments of the 1st
Brigade, serving to show what admirable marksmen

E

were in the ranks of the enemy. Indeed, it was confidently stated that many of the ermine hunters from
the north had been brought down and were attached
to the Russian army before Sebastopol.

In most of the parapets of the trenches, at the top
of the gabions, were double rows of sand-bags, and
these again were covered with earth; at intervals,
in order to permit more secure observation and to
allow our marksmen to be usefully employed, small
loop-holes were formed, and, according to the taste
or discretion of the field-officer commanding, a fire
might be kept up on the embrasures if any activity
prevailed, or on the clever skirmishers, or on the
diggers of the ambuscades, isolated in the first instance in couples, or singly, to work an ambush.

Through one of the sand-bag loop-holes a British
private had been firing with, as he fancied, indifferent
success, and therefore took a sergeant into consulta-
tion; the latter was judging the distance and looking
through the loop-hole, whilst the private, much inte-
rested, looked over the sergeant's shoulder. Nothing
could be seen of these two men above the parapets,
except perhaps the moving of the top of their forage
caps, but so judicious was the judgment and so excel-

lent the aim of a Russian rifleman, that a rifle shot entered the loop-hole, passed through the head of the sergeant and the throat of the private, killing both men.

As the small loop-hole was scarcely visible such a shot could only have been made by the marksman calculating where the face was from the slight circum stance of a cap being observed an inch or two over the parapet, breaking the regularity of the line of defence.   The two poor victims to such deadly aim were buried on the spot where they fell, and their arms and accoutrements carried back to camp.

On the return of the party with the dismal details of the death of the two men who had left their com- rades so short a time before, gloom and sadness pre- vailed in the small world of that regimental camp, the sergeant having been highly esteemed by both officers and men, the one the colour-sergeant of a company, and the private a man of some service and standing.

The French certainly understand the mode of giving effect to martial spectacles, but British ex- hibitions of the same kind are very tame.   In the neighbourhood of Lord Raglan's head-quarters, close to which some of the French cavalry were encamped, a most soul-inspiring scene took place on the 21st March. The occasion was one of promotion amongst the cavalry. The 1st and 4th Chasseurs d'Afrique, clad in light blue and silver and mounted on grey chargers, were drawn up in line, with a heavy regiment dressed in green, with the helmet and horse hair hanging down behind (now long discarded amongst us), mounted on strong Norman horses ; the latter corps had recently arrived with General Canrobert.

Nothing in appearance could exceed these three regiments ; the dragoons combined solidity, uniformity, and steadiness, and the chasseurs seemed made for the very purposes intended. The general was of course received with the usual compliments, and after gratefully acknowledging the honour, he proceeded along the front and rear of this long line, finally taking his place in the centre of the chasseur regiment on the right.

The names of the individuals to be promoted were then called out by the general of cavalry, and each, on being designated " au nom de l'Empéreur," chef-d'escadron, capitaine, lieutenant, or sous-lieutenant

galloped to the front, saluted the general command-
ing-in-chief, and then, completing a circle, joined the
squadron or troop to which he was appointed, the
band and trumpets playing at each nomination.

Thus Canrobert, with all the acting and attention
to ceremonial for which he was celebrated even
amongst his countrymen, and so representative of a
nation peculiarly devoted to the art of pleasing, went
through his part, and any individual present on that
day must admit that the French mode of conferring
promotion publicly, in presence of all concerned, is
far preferable to the cold English plan of the Gazette
and the Orders, where the man's name promoted is
scarcely noticed except by the officer's immediate
friends, or by those who partially reap the benefit.
The French by the very act impart a spirit of emula-
tion into their troops, which is utterly unknown to
the British.

The two sea-service mortars before alluded to
opened on the 31st March, but their performances
were anything but satisfactory. Their range was
said to be something like 5,000 yards, but many
fuses failed, the shells bursting in the air were a
serious infliction, the pieces falling close to our own

trenches, threatening death and destruction to our own troops.

There was little firing by the enemy between the 19th and 22d March, but on the night of the latter, between eight and nine, it became heavy and continuous. It was very dark, and the brigade was in momentary expectation of being ordered under arms.

CHAPTER IV.

Grand Sortie of the Russians—Captain Hedley Vicars—Lieutenant
Marsh's Presence of Mind—Success of the Allies—Real and
False Attacks—Robbing the Slain in the Heat of Action—A
Mummy, Swathed and Wrapped—A Two Hours' Armistice—
Terrible Shot—Rapid Change of Ownership.

THE fire continued, and the rattle of small arms told
us something was going on ; the peculiar howl, too,
of the Russians could be distinctly heard advancing
and receding. Wounded men also were dropping in,
and early on the 23d, at 1 a.m., an orderly was
sent round ordering us under arms at day-light
without sound of bugle ; on our falling in we found a
grand sortie had been made along the whole of our
lines. The enemy had attacked the French on the
right of our right attack, and the field-officer in command of our right attack, with some vague idea of
assisting our allies, weakened his left and withdrew his
men from the centre and right, and from our advance
works ; having done this, he advanced with his force,
or such as he could muster, was shortly afterwards

taken prisoner, and Lieutenant Jordan of the 34th was killed.

In the meantime the Russians, proceeding along the French trenches, reached those of the English, but not without a struggle. It was at the junction of the two that the gallant Hedley Vicars fell, as was supposed, wounded, but by the time he was carried to the battery in our first parallel he was dead.

Almost simultaneously with this attack on the right the enemy appeared in rear of a weak party of the rifle brigade on the extreme left of the right attack, where they had remained to guard the critical point where it terminates and looks down on the Woronzoff road. To the usual challenge the answer was, "Bueno Française," and the enemy immediately commenced firing, whilst at the same moment another party entered over the parapet at the centre of the "Old Advance," and proceeded to seize the 2-gun battery.

To the right of this again, communicating with the new parallel, was posted a party of the 7th and 33rd Regiments under Captain the Hon. C. Brown, who immediately led his men to the left against the

Russian party in the 2-gun battery ; in this he was
ably seconded by Lieutenant Marsh* of the 33rd Regiment.   A traverse intervened, the enemy on one side
and the British on the other, and whoever attempted
to pass the angle of the traverse was shot or
bayoneted.   Here Captain Brown was killed, receiv-
ing, besides the death shot, four or five wounds every
one of which would have been mortal.

Seeing how unfortunately matters stood, Lieutenant
Marsh, with a degree of cleverness and presence of
mind which would have done honour to an older
and more experienced soldier than he happened to be,
clambered up the side of the traverse and pushed
stones over on to the heads of the enemy.   Whilst
they in astonishment were looking about endeavouring to discover what was the matter, a party of the
7th, led by a gallant sergeant named Fisher,† carried

* Subsequently killed about 20th June, in unwisely endeavouring
to cross the open from point to point, instead of going a longer distance through the works.

† This man's services were such, that on several occasions he would
have ensured the position of an officer had he been sufficiently under
self-control to abstain from drink, and had he been better educated.
Wearing a good-conduct medal for gallantry, he subsequently, after
the war, took a free discharge rather than attend school, so that by
an attempt to force education the Queen's service lost a soldier
whose value in war it was impossible to estimate too highly.

the point, and being quickly joined by parties from other regiments, obtained possession of the position and commenced firing from the right, whilst a cross fire, poured in from the left, soon drove the Russians entirely out of the work known as the "Old Advance."

Success had also attended our allies and our own efforts on the right, the enemy retiring utterly discomfited.

Whilst the real attack was thus made on the allied right, (termed the British right attack, and on the French on the right again beyond, where considerable loss was sustained, several officers killed, and the colonel of the 34th English Regiment made prisoner), a false attack was carried on against the British left, —the covering party of the workers employed there, not being very forward, the enemy carried off the tools, such as picks and shovels, to the number of a couple of hundred, and made a more valuable prize in the person of Captain Montague, Royal Engineers, an excellent and enterprising officer, who was taken prisoner.

The attack on the right was led by an Albanian, —-he was killed in our works, and from his pockets, whilst the affair was going on, thirty gold pieces were abstracted by a soldier of the 34th Regiment.

All communities have their ideas of right and wrong; so it is with soldiers, even in the matter of despoiling the dead. The circumstance of the Albanian's body having been searched in the heat of action for plunder, was not only conduct directly opposed to an Article of War, but it gave rise to many unfavourable remarks amongst his comrades and the men of other regiments regarding the rapacious individual who thus obtained the thirty gold pieces.

It was said, but met with little credence, that the enemy held our work for half an hour.

The scene at daylight on the 23d was curious. Up beyond and about the ambuscades or rifle pits close to the Mamelon in front of the trenches, scattered numerously amongst the corpses, the red-breeched Zouaves could be distinguished. Here and there a red speck showed that some gallant Frenchman had fallen far in advance, repulsing the enemy. Along the whole front of the British right attack glasses were out, examining and speculating as to the different corpses, but more in search of that

of the Colonel of the 34th Regiment, who was supposed at the time to have been killed.

This officer was most careful of himself, and used
to proceed on duty to the trenches well provided
against the cold. Swathed and wrapped up like a
mummy, he always wore his red coat underneath
all—a practice more generally omitted. On the 22d
March he was as usual admirably clothed, and it was
stated subsequently that, being prodded with a
bayonet which did not penetrate through his numerous garments, and felled by the butt-end of a Russian
firelock, to which his skull was impervious, as no
further injury was inflicted, he was searched for spoil,
when, on his red coat being reached, he was discovered to be an officer, and was then carefully
conveyed away a prisoner. So the story runs, and
there seem no fair grounds for doubting it.

The 24th March was devoted to burying the dead,
and an armistice was proclaimed for two hours.
During this short time more than half those engaged
in the right attack availed themselves of the opportunity of seeing the Russians closer than at other
moments would have been desirable.

The enemy were of all sorts, from the swarthy

negro to the noble looking Greek. A certain line
of demarcation was kept, to which the corpses of
each side were brought, and received over from the
stretcher parties ; those belonging to the Russians
were borne away by them towards Sebastopol, whilst
those belonging to the English were taken to the
trenches by our soldiers.

Curiosity hunters, with pockets well lined, were
numerous—this "lining" was rapidly exchanged with
the men for useless lumber, and again the "lining"
was as quickly exchanged by the British soldier with
the French for some villanous French compound
in the shape of drink. All descriptions of missiles
were lying about. Bayonets scattered, loose cartridges and balls of every shape. Some were cutting
buttons, mementos for those far away, from some
unfortunate Russian corpse ; others, again, were examining the ground, and speculating on the extraordinary nature of the shot.

One description of shot, at first sight, appeared
capable of producing terrible effects ; but probably,
except at very close quarters, or at a short distance,
was really harmless. It was formed by connecting
two balls together by a twisted wire or spiral spring,

which, so connected and closing when rammed home
in the firelock or pistol, would occupy little space, but
would, the moment the muzzle was left on discharge,
be likely to inflict death and destruction amidst a
crowd in the trenches. Doubtless after a few yards
the balls by their own weight would separate, but
still, for the very short distance before separation, a
most deadly weapon was devised.

Hours soon fly, and Sir George Brown's assistant-
adjutant-general recalled loiterers, and announced the
armistice was closing. By three o'clock a gun occasionally fired showed that the strife had again commenced. And the busy crowd of adversaries, who,
for the moment, had become friends, disappeared
behind their respective defences intent only on
watching their mutual efforts for the destruction of
each other.

A bayonet, which served when stuck in the ground
as an admirable candlestick, the socket holding the
candles, with one or two of the destructive chain
cartridges alluded to, were the mementos we obtained
on the 22d of March.

Death, when one is employed before an enemy in the
field, can never be very unexpected, yet when it does

come it temporarily affects the survivors. A sale of the deceased officer's effects takes place, usually immediately after his burial, and, in the case of an officer killed in action, the whole business is over within forty-eight hours; the tent is then struck, to be re-pitched a few yards, nay, perhaps only a few feet from the original spot for a fresh occupant, and all goes on as if the one departed had never existed.

There are some exceptions, however. Captain Vicar's life and death have been published as an example to the world, and his memory is engraved in the hearts of many. The other captain who fell on the 22d March had a brother serving in the trenches of the left attack on the same night, but he was ignorant of the lamentable casualty which had occurred until relieved the following day.

CHAPTER V.

THE usual routine of trench duty continued, varied by tiresome and constant night alarms. At such times the brigade invariably fell in under arms, and sometimes were out two, three, and four times a night with uncertain intervals between, and the reader will understand how greatly we were harassed; but not so much, however, as a person accustomed nightly to a comfortable bed could imagine, for the human animal soon accommodates itself when in sound health to these watchings; it was surprising how quickly and how readily every individual turned out, and was again as quickly asleep. On the very young this nightly work soon told, especially on the boy officers and the recruits arriving with the drafts.

From guns probably sunk at an angle in the

ground, some shots thrown at very long ranges into the 3d Division Camp varied the monotony, fired no doubt in consequence of the enemy perceiving men digging in what happened to be the ditch for the electric telegraph.

Whenever the keen-eyed Russian saw the smallest semblance of work, whether building, carrying ammunition, or even piling gabions, fire was sure to be directed to the spot. And though a shot from a gun sunk as described could not be delivered with much accuracy, still a 32-pounder dropping unexpectedly into the midst of one's very camp gives an unpleasant thrill, and produces sensations of alarm.

Towards the end of March various circumstances led to the conclusion that the long-talked-of bombardment would shortly open. First the repairing and strengthening the parapets was persistently carried on at night. This was a duty entailing constant, severe, and harassing working parties, and sometimes heavy loss was sustained.

In this employment early in April Captain Bainbrigge, of the Royal Engineers, lost his life. The fire was very heavy and the shelling pretty accurate, —-after nearly completing the night's work he

F

had withdrawn the working parties of the line, but, in consequence of an uncalled-for remark from his immediate superior, he, with a corporal of Sappers, jumped up, as he expressed it, "just to square and finish the angles of an embrasure." A shell was seen in its flight, and Bainbrigge, who had been only a short time out, judging erroneously, shouted, "it will clear us." Fatal conclusion! Whilst the corporal jumped outwards from the work and escaped, the captain was struck and blown to atoms.

Very considerable supplies of ammunition at this time were brought up to the front, and the clearing out of the brigade and regimental hospitals, and transporting their inmates to Balaclava or on board ship, gave sure signs of the advent of terrible work at hand.

Much shelling from the enemy went on in the course of the 1st of April and following days. On the 4th it was more than usually severe. Notwithstanding this hard work, the indifferent fare, the shelling, the discomforts and anxieties, the Light Division races came off on the 7th, the Saturday between Good Friday and Easter Sunday. They were well attended, and would have ended cheerfully had it not been for a sad accident to two captains, —rival jockies at a hurdle race,—who, taking together the first fence, were unhorsed, fell, and appeared fatally injured ; in the course of a fortnight, however, both returned to their duty, but one was subsequently killed on the 18th of June.

The night of Easter Sunday had been wet, and the next morning, the 9th April, about five o'clock, a continued rolling fire of guns deadened though the noise was by the density of the atmosphere, announced the commencement of the long-looked-for bombardment.

Although expected yet, when it began, we were somewhat taken by surprise. Very late the previous night the order was given to the artillery, and it commenced it was said irrespective of weather, because the British Commander wished to keep faith with our allies, having promised the batteries should open on this day. It was added that information had been given by a deserter that the élite of the Russian gunners had gone to Eupatoria, and that the moment had been taken advantage of.

We subordinates were fairly puzzled ; the want of clearness in the atmosphere, and the rain falling

almost as heavily as in the tropics were enough of
themselves to prevent the fire being effective; besides
many of our advanced works and batteries were in-
complete. Independently of the unfortunate weather,
our fire was indifferent, and was responded to by an
occasional gun from the Malakoff, the Mamelon Verte,
or Gordon's Hill, or from the Redan.

Not the smallest effect seemed to be caused by our
shot. The rain was drenching, the Middle Ravine
leading to our covered way became a torrent, the
edges ten or twelve inches deep in the most abomin-
able mud, and the effluvium, arising probably from
some of the matter from the dead buried on each
side of the Ravine being washed down, was horrible.

The covered way itself and the trenches were in
some parts ponds, or deep and treacherous holes,—in
all a mixture of mud and stones. After such a
laborious walk it was not to be wondered at that
our fire was indifferent; the artillerymen were exhausted before they reached their guns, and before
their real work commenced; and when they came
off duty they were fairly pitiable objects, pale and
haggard. Eight hours on, and then the same number
off, were too much for any man to effectively work

heavy guns ; then too, from the time in camp must be deducted that occupied in going to and from the batteries. The fact is, there ought to have been thrice the number of artillery belonging to the siege train.

Towards dusk in the afternoon our fire slackened, and as soon as darkness had set in our mortars opened with shell. The two sea-service mortars, established on the Spur in front of the 2d Brigade, endeavoured to contribute their share, but many of these shells burst over our devoted heads, threatening destruction to friend instead of foe, and causing much more alarm to the British than to the Russians.

The practice, taken as a whole, was decidedly indifferent, an undue proportion bursting in mid-air, or closely following the discharge. But what wonder, when it was arranged that old materials should be used, and the contents of the Mediterranean magazines exhausted—*so that fuses made in* 1798, 1801, 1804, *and* 1812 *were actually employed in the great siege and second bombardment of Sebastopol in April* 1855 !

This, with damaged powder re-stored and then issued, would fully account for the admitted indifferent practice without the special cause that was assigned, the insufficient numbers of the artillery.

When morning broke (the 10th April), the night having passed with only one alarm of a sortie which caused us to stand to our arms, the mortar fire slackened and the guns again opened. Scarcely any reply was vouchsafed by the enemy, indeed a gallant young mate of the Naval Brigade, who was on duty with the seamen employed on the right of the artillery in Gordon's (21-gun) battery, went so far as to report that we had silenced the Malakoff. It sounded well and seemed correct. Alas! before the boy's return, for he had to go some distance, destruction amongst his men and fire from the presumed dismounted Malakoff guns, showed that the enemy's silence, far from being the effects of injury, was the result of design.

Subsequently, later in the day, the Russians certainly returned two shots for every one of the British. The guns worked by the seamen made fair practice— better than that of the artillery—but this is easily accounted for. The sailors, going on duty for twenty-four hours, formed a sort of cave for themselves, cooked their victuals on the spot, and, being divided into three watches, were constantly relieved without the drawback of being obliged to leave the battery, and go some distance to their camp.

Not the least interesting sight witnessed on the 10th of April was the British Fleet, the St Jean d'Acre leading, threatening the harbour and appearing as if about to enter. This feint did not answer, for the Russians were far too clever to allow their attention to be distracted by such a device ; but the sight of these moving masses, and in such numerical strength, is one never to be forgotten.

On the 12th April Captain Crofton, Royal Engineers, was severely wounded and died a few days afterwards, adding another to the victims belonging to this gallant corps.

The following night a very heavy fire of musketry was heard on the extreme left. This was caused by a successful endeavour on the part of the French to establish themselves and effect a lodgement near the Bastion du Mat. On the 16th the firing of the enemy was severe, and signalised by a misfortune to the British, for in the afternoon the magazine, at what was termed the Eight-Gun Battery immediately in front of the Twenty-one Gun Battery, blew up. By this disaster seven or eight artillery-men lost their lives, and several more were severely injured. An explosion of such a description for the moment elates the adversary, and the Russians signified their satisfaction by opening fire briskly from the often-thought silenced Malakoff.

With the explosion of this magazine the second bombardment of Sebastopol may be said to have terminated ; for, though we continued to fire occasionally, orders were issued to slacken and merely to fire one gun every half hour.

An interesting reconnaissance was made on the 19th. The Turks under Omar Pasha went out on the right of Balaclava, whilst our cavalry, with a few infantry and horse artillery, on the left proceeded towards the Tchernaya. The result was very satisfactory, it being ascertained that there was no force of the enemy on the east side of the British and Allied positions.

A rifle pit or ambuscade had for some time been established in a spot near the left advance of the right attack, which materially interfered with our approaches towards the Quarries, and absolutely was formed at the very point where the next angle of our zig-zag would come. It was therefore essential that we should dislodge the inmates and take possession of it, together with another ambuscade nearly adjoining.

This duty fell to the lot of Lieut.-Colonel Egerton, of the 77th Regiment. He was the next Lieutenant-Colonel on the Rolster. Accordingly, about three hundred men of the above corps, and nearly a similar number from the 33d Regiment, under a field officer, were detailed and marched down to the trenches, under the name of a " Reserve," but really to carry out the business of taking the pits.

As soon as darkness fell the column, which had been divided into three companies for attack, support, and reserve (the last remaining within the trenches) advanced, and easily dislodged the enemy, taking a few prisoners. Some of the 77th were left to hold our acquisition, whilst the remainder retired to our works, of course on the *qui vive.*

In taking the pits Captain Lempriere, of the 77th, an especial regimental favourite, was mortally wounded, and died in a few minutes. He was perhaps the smallest man in the army, and was carried back in the arms of Colonel Egerton, who exclaimed, " Could they not spare you, my poor boy ! "

The Russians immediately commenced a heavy fire of musketry, under cover of which it was expected they would advance and endeavour to re-take these pits. Consequently everybody was on the look-out, and Colonel Egerton, who had previously been slightly wounded in the groin, was constantly on the parapet endeavouring to discern through the darkness. In doing this he was struck through the head, and fell dead. Nearly at the same moment the foe advanced and re-took one of the rifle pits; with this temporary advantage, for they evacuated it the following day, they were satisfied.

Though successful, the retention of the pit (subsequently designated Egerton's Pit), was dearly purchased, and the night was unfortunate, for Captains Baines and Owen, of the Royal Engineers, belonging to the right attack, were dangerously wounded, the first, as it turned out, mortally; the second losing his leg above the knee.

The funeral of the fallen on the 19th took place two days after, on Saturday the 21st. It was attended by Lord Raglan in person, and nearly every officer of the Light Division off duty, besides most of the generals and commanding officers. The Colonel, with his friend and comrade Captain Lempriere, were laid amongst their men, close together, in the graveyard of the second brigade, on the left of the Woronzoff Road, leading past and close to the picquet house.

In abilities Colonel Egerton was superior to most; in winning the affections of his subordinates unrivalled; in devotion to the Queen's service not to be outdone; withal his wit and conversation were such that the hours of an individual whose tour of duty brought him into proximity with this lamented officer in the trenches, slipped by, and were recurred to with pleasure. The army by his death lost the most promising officer certainly of his rank and standing.

Although on the night of the 20th April a ship or two got in pretty close and were supposed to have done some damage, the bombardment completely ceased on that day. We were very nearly in the same position as before it commenced on the 9th of April. It is true that most likely we had inflicted considerable loss of life, but there was no material injury observable in the enemy's works.

What the ships may have done of course cannot be known. It was the practice for a ship or two to approach as near as possible at night, going in by compass, and salute the north and north-west part of the town with shot or shell, whichever suited the taste or armament of the vessel. Such messengers, unexpectedly reaching a locality considered safe, or where troops happened to be, must have created panic and produced considerable effect on the Russian morale.

That shortly after the 9th of April an assault might have been attended with success appears probable, because, at the moment, the garrison of Sebastopol was unusually weak; but within seven days the usual reliefs, with their long trains of mules, were seen arriving on the north side. Whether with a view to prove Russian nonchalance or not it is difficult to say, but during some of the heaviest fire the softest strains of music were wafted across from the enemy's band on the north side of the harbour. The music was from brass instruments alone, and the more pleasing because unexpected.

CHAPTER VI.

THE first of May in the temperate zone is held to be
the commencement of summer. It burst forth in the
Crimea with all the luxuriance of a climate which
had been shut up by frost and snow. As the rain
had been almost tropical, so, on the other hand,
vegetation seemed as rapid as on the breaking up of
a Canadian winter. In one night, through the brown
substance which had once been grass, whole patches
of verdure arose, the produce of hidden bulbs or
roots. The ravines especially attracted attention,
and our eyes feasted on the sight of flowers known
at home.

The view of the valley of the Tchernaya was rich
in the extreme, and the pasture most inviting. There

were our greedy and indefatigable allies mowing and
gathering in the grass to the utmost limits of their
advanced sentries, whilst we looked on with envy,
and with feelings something akin to those felt towards
our enemy.   Our friends the French, though they
allowed their own people to graze within their
sentries, took good care the English should not enjoy
the boon.   Certainly there was little courtesy evinced
towards us.   Even in the matter of sporting a
Frenchman was allowed, with dogs and gun, to pass
a forbidden spot, whilst the English officer would be
arrested by the words, " Il est defendu," and yet see
the brother sportsman and ally knock over a hare
within sixty or eighty yards of him.

Such incidents as these created no pleasant feeling.
Complaining was of little use.   If a report to our
brigadier Sir William Codrington was followed up
and represented, still it only ended in disappointment,
for, should the delinquent's regiment be ascertained,
he was sheltered, and promises and apologies were
the only result.   Yet on the very next occasion the
same thing took place.   Sometimes the French guard
would assert that the English officer had declined to
ccmply with the sentry's orders (a great military

offence), or that bad language had been used; in fact, in whichever way the matter was represented there was usually a counter complaint and the Englishman went to the wall.

To an officer in uniform visiting the French trenches nothing could exceed the civility and attention shown to him. There was nothing then that could militate against the interests of our gallant allies, and they were glad to enjoy a little chat, though it was difficult to extract from them any information either as to their casualties, or any other matter connected with their proceedings.

A party of five of us, making a trip one day to the extreme left and thence to Kamiesch, fell upon a portion of the Legion Etrangère. Not one amongst us knew a French officer, but we stumbled on an individual, half an Englishman half a Frenchman, who not only was most polite but showed us where to obtain permission, and then conducted us to a raised work termed the "Observatoire."

From this position an excellent view was obtained of the French works on the west or allied left, and of the beaches on the south-west side of Sebastopol. The ruins of the church of St Wladimir and its desecrated churchyard, the scene of nightly and bloody conflicts, was here close to us. From this point the view of Fort Constantine was probably the best, and also that of the large building in the middle of the town, which, whether library, theatre, or what answers to the French Hotel de Ville, to this moment we have not been able to determine.

Our friend, whose regiment was located on the extreme left of the French army and who had been constantly on duty and employed in the construction of the works, was able, and, as it happened, willing to afford us every information. His career had been an eventful one, and he himself was a singular illustration of the manner and of the men composing this corps. After exchanging civilities, and reciprocating his invitation, we bade adieu to Mons. de Rivière. Whether he lived to benefit by our proffered hospitality, or whether he perished in the mortal strife which shortly afterwards took place near this part of the position, remains a mystery.

After various attempts, the French about this time were successful in taking and holding an outwork to the left of the British and close to the Bastion du Mat. They effectually beat the enemy out of their own work, but the latter was determined not to relinquish the post without another struggle, and on the following day, at an unusual and unexpected time between three and four in the afternoon, under cover of a most tremendous fire, the enemy endeavoured to retake the work, but without success.

The casualties on this occasion were enormous, and it was currently rumoured that the very same Russian corps which had been driven out the previous night was called on to wipe out the disgrace and recover the lost ground in the day-light.

Close to the British head-quarters a review, in the ordinary acceptation of the word, of French cavalry was held on the 6th of May.   There was no attempt at manœuvring, the troops merely paraded in line, broke into columns of squadrons, and marched home. The Chasseur d' Afrique and the "Dragons," answering to our heavy dragoons, were the regiments.   The spectators were more numerous than the men reviewed. British officers were there in every variety of costume and mounted on every description of animal. The staff of French generals was more than usually numerous.

Early in the month of May the command of the Light Division changed hands. Sir George Brown,

G

accompanied by his staff (the only part of the division which he took with him), proceeded to Kertch in command of some two thousand men; Sir William Codrington succeeded, and the change of commanders was appreciated by both officers and men.

Whilst the gallant Sir George was fidgetty and nervous, turning out his troops at the most trifling noise of firing, frequently four and five times a night, Sir William Codrington never spared himself, and invariably, before issuing orders for the division to get under arms, reconnoitred, and ascertained if there were any necessity for so doing. So that, whilst one general spared himself at the expense of his troops, the other spared the troops at the expense of his own rest.

Soldiers very quickly discern, value, and respect such sacrifice. And they look up to the brigadier who, instead of depending on subordinate staff-officers for information whilst serving in the face of an enemy, trusts to his own eyes. At the most uncertain hours, day and night, mounted on his well known grey, might Sir William be met on his rounds.

A practice which more than once had told with effect and caused panic in our trenches, was unsuccessful on the night of the 10th of May. We were become by that time numerically stronger, and were enabled to exercise a greater degree of vigilance. Our wily foes were in the habit of lying on their stomachs, and thus crawling round the angles of the zigzags. For this service men were selected for their cleverness and address.

Having attained the rear of our advance parties, they either reconnoitred and retired, or entered the works ; or perhaps, if there was a sortie in combination, they opened fire, which was the more distressing because it could neither be returned by the British in the parallels, nor by the party lining the zig-zag advances without the danger of sacrificing friend as well as foe.

On the night in question the Russians were discovered in the very act of endeavouring to creep to the rear, and the flashes and light caused by the bursting of our shells disclosed the enemy's columns prepared and drawn up evidently ready to attack us.

From a sortie which was made on the left, and from the fact of the columns and their advance parties having been discovered, it may be concluded that an extensive operation was intended. But whether a feint or a real attack, the enemy paid off the fortunate discovery on the right by a very heavy combined fire of shot and shell.

It is difficult to convey to the mind an adequate description of the grandeur and beauty of a heavy fire, commonly called at that time a duel at night. The flashes were so brilliant that, for a moment, figures were distinctly visible that were shrouded again the next in utter darkness. The fuse of the shells in mid-air betrayed the course of these missiles; whilst occasionally light-balls discharged showed for several minutes everything around.

Such a scene occurred on the 13th of May, when the enemy strove hard on the left against the French on the extreme left of the British. Every sort of combustible lighted up the sky. There were shells of all sorts and sizes. Then there were bouquets, facetiously so called. These consist of a number of small shells or grenades enclosed in a large one, which, on exploding, scatters not only destruction in its vicinity, but the small shells like so many serpents, with the impetus imparted from the parent shell, insidiously go on bursting at uncertain intervals, some on the ground, some in the air, rendering all calculations erroneous, and no locality except a bomb-proof secure.

These missiles were plentifully exchanged. At moments twenty shells were in the air at once, and then at times the Russians could be noticed, with spades and other implements, endeavouring to extinguish an obstinate light-ball.

The time chosen for an attack or duel is always a critical hour in war, particularly during a siege. It was usually in the interval after the moon had set, and before the break of day. That (in the trenches) valued orb had set late, consequently the darkness only lasted for about some ninety or a hundred minutes; but the blaze and the darkness alternating rendered the latter even more opaque,—it was as if a hundred Vauxhalls had been condensed into the smallest possible space. The scene cannot be realised except by an eye-witness.

Orders for the preparation of water-bags, and sundry directions about buttresses, led us to the belief, about the 17th of May, that either a division was to be despatched to another point, or that the British army was to take the field, and it is not too

much to assert that all hearts panted for something
active and creditable to be attempted.

From our plateau we could see the luxuriant grass,
and the smiling valley of the Tchernaya, the advanced posts of our allies gathering the fine pro-
vender, and many French officers' horses grazing.
In the same way with the shooting : whilst the
French permitted their own people to collect forage,
and their own animals to graze, not an English
officer's horse was allowed to pass their sentries.

The sight of the pasture added additional zeal and
energy to the packing up and despatching warm
clothing. The sun rose with great power, almost
such as is felt in the tropics, yet with the fine
weather health did not come. Dropping cases of
cholera occurred ; men that had passed through the
bullets of the enemy unharmed were suddenly cut
off or smitten by this fell disease. Amongst those
most lamented was Major Norton of the 88th Regiment. He attended a sale which took place on the
19th of May, at twelve o'clock, was directly afterwards attacked by cholera, and died early the next
morning. He had been the life and soul of the
division races, loving the sport solely for its own

sake, and his all but sudden death was much felt, casting gloom throughout the division.

An anecdote illustrative of Lord Raglan's kindly nature may be told in connection with Norton. It chanced that shortly after the landing at Old Fort, Norton, then a captain, was seized with illness, and accompanied the army placed upon an araba. No shelter was to be obtained, and Lord Raglan, on the advance to the Bulganac, observing the invalid had him conveyed to the farm-house occupied by himself and staff. Whilst the aides-de-camps were fully occupied with their own preparations and wants, and unable to give attention to their sick comrade, Lord Raglan himself ministered to his comfort. His lordship sat by his couch, and brought tea and refreshments with his own hand. To this most kind consideration Captain Norton was indebted for convalescence, and gained sufficient strength to lead his company into action at the battle of the Alma.*

The races got up by the 4th Division of the army took place on the 22d of May, when the horse of a gallant French chasseur all but won the prize. On the impromptu course might be seen admirals, generals,

* This statement was made by Captain Norton to the writer.

Turks, Sardinians, and French, whilst but few ladies graced the spectacle. There was one, however, the wife of a hussar paymaster, who could hardly be called a stranger or visitor, for at all times and seasons, in pleasure or depression, amidst the tumult of bombardment or on the field of carnage, attended by an escort of beaux, she might be found.

On this day the French Commander-in-chief inspected a force of infantry consisting of two battalions of the line, one of Zouaves and one of Chasseurs de Vincennes. Without the stiffness, or that which our allies would term the "solidité" of the English, as these troops marched past they presented a martial confidence and aspect seldom seen. The Englishman merely follows the lessons of drill and obedience, but the Frenchman is almost individually filled with enthusiasm.

Whether this inspection was preparatory to the business of the night, or of that which took place some two days subsequently, on the 25th of May, we never learned, but about nine at night some of the heaviest fire which had been heard during the siege commenced and continued until twelve. It was entirely confined to the French on the extreme left, and they then made an attack in force on the works near the Quarantine Harbour.

Whether by chance or through treachery a large body of Russians was ready to receive them, and a most severe contest took place. In addition to the enemy's troops being thus prepared, several Russian ships had been moored in such a manner that their guns could be brought to bear on the reverse of the Russian defences, so that most likely a traitor had given information. The strife was most intense; twice the French carried the works, and twice they were driven back. The third time, notwithstanding the fire of the ships on the intruders, our gallant allies retained possession, but only temporarily, for about two the next morning, after a renewed contest, they evacuated the work.

Either from the distance of the enemy's ships, or from the failure of the signals, the guns of the enemy's vessels continued their fire on the interior of the defences after the French had evacuated them and thus caused great carnage amongst their own troops.

The Guards Imperial, with the 14th, 18th, and 46th of the line, formed a portion of the troops engaged in this affair, which was conducted under the orders of Pelissier, the future commander-in-chief of the French army.

The casualties were said to number fifteen hundred, but with what degree of truth is uncertain. A sad calamity, causing considerable loss, happened on this occasion. A company of the voltigeurs of the Guard, newly arrived and unacquainted with the intricacies of the trenches, mistook their position in the attack, and paid bitterly for the want of definite instructions and real knowledge ; they were slaughtered nearly to a man, for, out of ninety-six that went into action, three only returned.

Later in the morning the French again renewed the attack, and this time with success, for the whole line of ambuscades, from the Bastion du Mat to the Quarantine remained in their hands.

From the preparations each had made, both French and Russians imagined treachery and spies had been at work. The former found a strong unexpected force ready to receive their attack, with the guns of the ships brought to bear upon them, whilst rumour accounted for these unlooked-for preparations by the statement that, this night, nay, at the very moment the French attack was made the Russians were ready for a sortie.

CHAPTER VII.

To celebrate the Queen's birthday, a grand review
was intended to be held on the 24th May, but the
weather being oppressive, and the infantry fully
occupied with their laborious duties in the trenches,
it was confined to the artillery and the cavalry.

The 10th Hussars and 12th Lancers, just arrived
from India, and of considerable numerical strength,
were each divided into three squadrons of 112 ; two
squadrons of the 10th Hussars were formed into a
regiment, two squadrons of the 12th Lancers into
another ; and a third regiment was composed of a
squadron each from the 10th and 12th, and the
heterogeneous materials, the sad remnants of the 4th

and 13th Light Dragoons, with those of the 17th Lancers and 8th and 11th Hussars. These troops made a fine light cavalry brigade.

The "Heavies" consisted of the remains of the 4th and 5th Dragoon Guards, the 1st, 2d, and 6th Dragoons, numbering 446. These, with a couple of troops of the Royal Horse Artillery, and the two heavy 24-lb. batteries just arrived from England, with their guns drawn by twelve horses four abreast, made a splendid sight. The strength in all must have been 2,100 mounted men. They were drawn up in line, the left resting very near the Monastery of St George, to await the arrival and inspection of Lord Raglan.

Punctual to the hour named, ten o'clock, his lordship came to the appointed rendezvous, and nearly at the same time Omar Pasha, who, at the review, rode on the right of Lord Raglan. He appeared of middle height, sunburnt and pale, spare in person, of intellectual countenance, and was dressed in a simple blue and gold tunic, wearing a star, ribbon, and order. A gold plate with diamonds glittered in front of his red fez cap. Occasionally forgetting he was not supreme, he would lift his right hand with one finger extended, either as a mark of admiration or the reverse, towards some portion of the troops.

The French Commander caused some delay. On arrival the lamented Lord Raglan, having tucked the reins of his horse under his stirrup, took off his cocked hat, bowed low, and thus received the plebeian, plump, short-cropped General Pelissier, the new and energetic French commander-in-chief.

The three Commanders, followed by their respective escorts and numerous suites, the British General, with Omar Pasha on his right and Pelissier on his left, passed down the line. Returning, they took up a position marked by a flag-staff, and the lines, breaking into columns of squadrons, marched past.

All eyes, at least most British eyes, were intent on the two regiments—the 10th Hussars and the 12th Lancers, and indeed no cavalry in the world could well surpass them, either in appearance or steadiness. Though mounted on smaller animals, the description of horses ridden by the 10th Hussars seemed well up to the weight; and both regiments, being of the Indian strength, and much greater than that of the ordinary English cavalry regiments serving with the army, must have taken the foreigners by surprise, and cre-

ated a favourable impression, especially after the small
bodies they had been accustomed to be shown as
British regiments.

The 24-lb. batteries, too, were greatly talked of.
The horses, twelve to each gun, four abreast, were
superb, but it was observed, if a stray shot disabled either of the two in the centre, much embarrass-
ment would be caused. The opinion, too, was
general, that eighteen pounder guns would have been
an improvement, nearly as effective, and the weight
and impedimenta of ammunition to be carried would
have been considerably lessened.

It was shortly after we had witnessed, with some
pride, two effective regiments of cavalry, worthy of
the nation, and likely to be more serviceable than the
squadrons we English denominate regiments, we
heard our civil rulers at the War Department had it
in contemplation to reduce the 10th Hussars and 12th
Lancers to the strength of the miserable numbers
of an ordinary cavalry regiment—on the plea of
economy (but really and ultimately at greater cost) ;
it was proposed to disband or transfer the surplus of
effectives who had been taught by discipline to act
thoroughly together, to scatter them under diffe-

rent heads, to undergo a new system, or perhaps to be drafted away to some newly-raised land transport or other corps.

If the civil authorities who govern the army would only listen to, or profit by, experience, or could be made to understand the much greater proportionate value of a body of men accustomed to act together under one commander, than the same numbers split into smaller divisions under different commanders, and of course not identified by an exactly similar system, they would long hesitate before venturing to reduce regiments such as the two Indian cavalry regiments were, or as many corps are on arriving in Great Britain from the colonies. By so doing, they impair the efficiency which time and discipline have made, without adding to that of the body to which the soldier is drafted.

If it is essential to the finances to reduce the numbers of our army, it should invariably be accomplished by ceasing to recruit, which is a safe and gradual measure ; not by the cruel and ungracious practice of discharge.*

* Discharges by reduction are thus arranged. There are three classes :—

1st Class.—Weak and sickly men.

Cavalry and artillery take a considerable period to become even respectable or fit to work together, and men not thoroughly taught, bad as they are in the other branches of the service, are in these worse than useless. They not only are incumbrances themselves, but they bring others in addition. For, unable to satisfy their own wants, they have in the one case horses, in the other guns, horses, and harness demanding their constant attention.

Just before the war in the Crimea broke out the

2d Class—Bad characters.
3d   „   Soldiers who are desirous of purchasing, or obtaining free discharges by indulgence.

By discharging the first you throw on the world a number of helpless men, many of whom, having lost their health by serving in the colonies, are incapable of earning a livelihood, and fall a burden on their respective parishes.

By discharging the second, you cast on the public a number of irreclaimable characters whom even military discipline has failed to reform ; if they were so disposed, they have no occupation in civil life, because probably their original one has made such progress that they no longer know it. Many live by begging, and prey upon the benevolent, more especially on the country clergy, who readily believe the wildest and most improbable tales. The discharge of such men, unless of long service, offers a premium to misconduct.

The third class, being fully trained soldiers, are allowed (in nine cases out of ten) to injure themselves by paying money for their discharge, and this permission also entails heavy loss to the public. As a matter of public profit, allowing a man to purchase his discharge any time within four months from the date of his enlistment is the only course to ensure it.

15th Hussars arrived in England from India. Composed of soldiers of from five to fifteen, and even twenty years' service, it was numerically very strong. Yet, disregarding the aspect of affairs, every encouragement was given to these valuable men to take their discharge, in other words, to fall generally a burden on their parishes for the sake of paltry and momentary economy. Within a few months such disciplined cavalry soldiers would have been most valuable, and an immense saving would have accrued, because the bounty having been raised we were paying very highly for the raw material in the shape of recruits ; even any of the soldiers of the 15th Hussars, finding their former occupation in civil life gone, again obtained the bounty on re-enlisting the same as the new recruit.

Therefore such sudden, ill-digested reductions as have been carried out during the last twenty years, with the view of leading the country to believe economy is effected because the numerical strength of the army is less, are in truth the grossest species of financial extravagance and political folly. Simply to cease recruiting for a longer time would more gradually and systematically lower the numbers, and the

H

abundance of men fitted for recruits which would follow the stoppage would enable Government, when men were wanted, to reduce the amount of the bounty.

On the morning of the 25th of May the long expected advance into the valley of the Tchernaya took place. The plateau on which the British and part of the French were located has often been described. It is doubtful if any description can realise the actual position, for the circular platform lies on precipitous rocks, and the slopes running into the valley are very irregular, affording no certain tracks by which the valley could easily be reached.

The allied encampment was on an extensive undulating plateau intersected partly by ravines on the northern or Sebastopol side, on the north-east, eastern, and south-east, then gradually descending towards the south by the slopes on the southern portion leading into the valley of Balaclava by Kadikoi.

On all sides it was pretty strongly intrenched. Batteries on the east overlooked the river and Tchernaya valley separating us from the Inkerman cliffs. The mountainous nature of the country beyond this, running to the south and south-east of the ruins of Inkerman, afforded a natural and formidable defence to the enemy. Concealed batteries were established on some of the opposite heights, and guns had occasionally been fired by the enemy across the valley into the (British) Second Division lines and encampment prior to its removal from that part of the allied position called " Inkerman"—not where the battle of Inkerman was fought, but a little to the rear.

Where the Woronzoff road fell into the valley, occupied at this period by the French in force, batteries and intrenchments had been constructed, and their advance posts were thence pushed forward. Still when the French parties proceeded too far, whether to water horses, or to secure more tempting herbage, a plunging shot or two from the enemy would remind them that their excursion might possibly not be harmless.

Towards the river on its left bank, continuing along the Woronzoff road, the grounds gradually ascend, and a succession of hills, "Morues," and Mamelons rise in the valley. Through the gorge of one of these runs the Woronzoff road, and descending crosses the aqueduct to the Traktu bridge, where in the summer the river is generally fordable. Higher up

the river, perhaps a couple of miles to the southward
and eastward, is a ford, and immediately opposite on
the right bank are the luxuriant orchards and villages
of Tchorgoun, overhung by precipitate cliffs. The
aqueduct, which runs parallel with the Tchernaya's
left bank, forms a very considerable obstacle and
an admirable defence immediately above the bridge
where the hills and heights overlook the river.

Thus a force established on the left bank above the
Traktu has two lines for an enemy to overcome,
first the river and then the aqueduct.

A large body of French descended from the dreary
plateau about eleven o'clock on the night of the 24th
of May, and rested below. At the first blush of
dawn they advanced, supported by numerous columns,
and gradually the whole valley was filled with French
troops steadily approaching the river. As soon as
the bridge was passed, the right, looking towards
the east, was occupied by the Sardinians. Near
Kamara and in front of it, Captain Thomas's troop of
horse artillery and several Sardinian battalions took
up their position.

Little resistance was offered by the enemy. A
redoubt, apparently held by a few Cossacks some

distance beyond the right bank of the river, was easily captured by the Zouaves in advance, but some shots from the heights to the left of the French, falling into the said redoubt, showed it was no desirable place to hold.

Riding along we forded the river at Tchorgoun, whence a few shots were fired from a battery which was immediately afterwards abandoned. But the French soon had their light guns up and fired some rounds towards the enemy, who might be seen on the heights looking down on Tchorgoun. The village itself was not entered further than by pushing forward some skirmishers, who were shortly withdrawn, but the underground dwelling of the Russian troops near the battery, which offered but a trivial resistance, was thoroughly ransacked.

It was amusing to see the French soldiers laden with spoil, some with boots, others with chairs, one with a kitten, another with a puppy, in fact every conceivable article.

Here we rested with the French guns, and admired the village and trees with the river meandering below us. Situated as Tchorgoun is, in a hollow with hills and cliffs on every side except that near the river, the French, having made a successful reconnaissance, had gained their object, and it would have been attended with considerable risk and no really useful result to have dislodged the enemy from the heights beyond and looking down on Tchorgoun. It was most consolatory to find the lines of the allied army extended to the Tchernaya.

Ascending a steep hill on the North of Tchorgoun (a desirable post for observation), we there found the French General-in-chief Pelissier, with generals of division Canrobert and Espinasse assembled. The first and last named wore over their uniform the white arab caïque,* to guard against the heat. Looking back from this spot towards Kamara were the artillery ; below, on the left bank of the Tchernaya, French cavalry, with a picquet on the right bank covering the ford, on the advanced videttes ; close to us were the Zouaves, and the plain of Balaclava was covered with troops, Sardinians, French, and Turks. In some places tents were erected as if the inmates had been located on the spot for months.

The spoil of the day was confined to a few prisoners,

---

* A circular cloak, with falling hood behind to cover the head and cap. There is a hole in the centre through which the head of the wearer passes.

and a large quantity of trash in the shape of paper
and accounts, a couple of guns, and a few horses and
carts. Wherever the main body might have been,
the few Russians occupying the redoubts had evidently hurried off in great haste, for there were un-
mistakable signs of flight ; even loaves and pieces of
fresh brown bread, parts of the day's rations.

The zest displayed by the Zouaves in advancing
was somewhat curious ; it was like the sportsman in
search of game. All nations belong to this corps,
and it was understood that at one period, on their
first organisation, many were volunteers from the
Legion Etrangère. It was our fortune to halt
with the batallion of Zouaves who were furthest
in advance. They had just discomfited their few
opponents, and were halted awaiting orders whether
to proceed, or to retire to, the left bank of the
Tchernaya.

An unfortunate Cossack or two had been killed,
and the remarks of the Zouaves were singular, but
extremely characteristic. One fellow had taken away
a Russian's medal, another his coat, and so on ; a third
pronounced their opponents "invalids," and worth
nothing, they were so old. Somewhat thoughtlessly

expressing surprise at the deliberate confidence with
which the Zouave pronounced upon the age, the man
observed, "Oh! we know it by the teeth—they have
few teeth." A Zouave came up and joined the conversation in good English. He said he had been to
London constantly, and was then a servant.

The most friendly disposition was evinced towards
us, yet nothing would tempt the Zouave corporal to
part with the medal he had taken from the dead.
This was unusual, for generally, both French and
English troops were glad to turn their spoil into
current coin, whether English, Russian, French, or
Turkish. In stating thus the kindly disposition
shown to two British officers who joined the Zouaves,
there is no intention by any means to assert that our
"friends," if we had been encamped near them,
would not have found our horses conveniently loose,
and have taken possession of them or of any other
article upon which they could lay their hands,
according to their ordinary practice,—they recognised no difference between "meum and tuum."

Now that the position was opened to the Tchernaya we were returning towards the plateau in high
spirits, exhilarated by the ride, and much pleased at

the prospect of future short and easy journeys to Balaclava. Each step of the horse made the air redolent with the sweet odours of the wild flowers, and to those who for months, tantalised by the distant view of grass, had been unable to touch or to wander through the luxuriant verdure, there was enough to excite the most phlegmatic disposition.

As we rode we came up to a poor Russian, certainly a non-combatant, just taken prisoner. From fear or from illness he was a wretched object, and was at once seized. By signs he endeavoured to explain he could not walk.

With troops doctors are generally at hand, and there were plenty with us. It was soon found he was suffering from an attack of cholera. Quickly the French had a cariole, and in it, though preferring to remain, the prisoner was obliged to mount. A little hesitation on his part drew from a French soldier a pretty heavy slap to hasten his movements, at the same time observing, " Ne faites pas le bête." Thinking bayonets looked unpleasant, and a disagreeable prick from one might follow, he got in.

On reaching the Traktu bridge across the Tchernaya we met hosts of English officers hastening down, but too late for the object in view—all was finished; still there was a military lesson to be learned. The French, immediately after crossing the river (knowing that their advance posts would be thrown forward from the left bank across the bridge), had already begun their defences, scarping the bank and high ground so that, even if the enemy forced a passage, he would find other difficulties to overcome, and a still further most formidable impediment beyond, the aqueduct running along the side of the hill.

This crossed, the still rising ground afforded advantages of no inconsiderable value to the allies. But it was over such defences the Russians contrived to advance, reach, and surprise our ally at the battle of the Tchernaya. No mean feat, considering the commanding position held by the French.

As before observed, across the valley on the range of hills or ridge about south-east of the ruins of Inkerman, in the cliffs the Russians had established several concealed and invisible batteries. From these they endeavoured to stay the progress of the French as they passed the bridge. Fortunately the guns were of small calibre, and the mortars inconsiderable. The shells mostly burst short in mid-air, and although the shot came occasionally much too close, it was evident there was no certainty in the firing; the French therefore could rest in peace, free from danger arising from the batteries established on the left bank of the Tchernaya.

On the high ground where the Woronzoff Road descends through the gorge, close to where the mutilated and wounded might be expected to pass after the recent reconnaissance, amongst a host of men, was Mrs D——. She had evidently ridden out in haste, and her graceful person figured in a scene where she could boast, if it were a subject worthy of boasting, that she was sole representative of her sex.

CHAPTER VIII.

AT six in the morning of Whit-Sunday, the 27th of
May, shortly after divine service had been celebrated,
the division was suddenly turned out to give three
cheers for the first substantial success obtained
during many months. The news had arrived of the
taking of Kertch, and its occupation ; with this was
coupled the victorious results gained by the squadron
in the Sea of Azoff, under Captain Lyons. Each
division turned out in succession, and the cheering
was most vociferous.

Of course these cheers reached the besieged, and, in addition to the loss sustained, must have had a most depressing effect on the enemy in Sebastopol. The noise made by the gallant 88th, long continued, was in itself sufficient to awaken inquiry, and each regiment, though perhaps not so loud in acclamation, cordially responded to the occasion.

The news was indeed most cheering, and calculated, with the additional freedom recently obtained by the extension of the allied lines as far as the Tchernaya, to raise the drooping spirits of the least sanguine. It was evident the Russians were now so far shut in, as to be compelled to depend for their future supplies entirely upon those brought overland from the North, and the chief source whence, we had good reason to believe, they had hitherto obtained their vast supply of provisions was effectually stopped by our success at Kertch. Besides this, access from the eastern part of the harbour was now in a manner arrested by the occupation of the valley by the French.

It must, however, be confessed that some hardship was felt in the Light Division because its General did not take even one of its companies upon the Kertch

expedition. Engaged in every action, by its fierce
determination, its very blood and bone had overcome
and driven the enemy from such a position as the
Alma, and had won honour and renown for its
General, who, forgetting he commanded a division,
led and fought them like a simple grenadier.
Having borne the unparalleled hardships of the
Crimean winter, holding an extended line with
numbers totally insufficient, but still successfully
maintaining the credit of the British name, yet this
division was left to wither in manning the wretched
trenches of the right attack.   No relief was given,
no change took place.

The French, Sardinians, and Turks now held the
valley of the Tchernaya. A few sickly batteries of
British artillery were also encamped between the
Tchernaya and the lines of Kadikoi, sent there in
the hope that the change of air might drive the
cholera from amongst the men, and that the rich
grass and herbage would assist in curing the plague
of mange which very pertinaciously clung to the
horses.

The Traktu bridge and the ford under Tchorgoun
were the limits to our wanderings. At the former

the French stopped all enterprising visitors who
wished to pass, and on the right bank with the
Sardinians a picquet of dragoons barred further progress at the latter.   But the privilege of bathing in
the stream, a healthful luxury to man and horse, was
open, and was enjoyed in a manner that only people
who have been without a bath for months can appreciate.

In the beginning of June the force in the Crimea
must have been nearly as follows :—in round numbers about two hundred and sixty thousand men,
composed of

French, ...	170,000
Turks, ...	45,000
Sardinians, . . .	15,000
British, ...	32,000

Of these, as to equipment, material, arms, men and
organisation the Sardinians, taken as a whole, were
the most perfect.   Perfection itself in military matters
is often assigned by theorists to the French, but how
very far from the truth is the actual practice of our
gallant allies.   Their discipline is lax in the extreme,
and in the ranks the officers, of the same class with

the men, do not carry much weight or authority.
With the British that which would be considered a
crime, is overlooked by the French.   There was not
a regimental camp that Zouaves did not visit with a
view to robbery or plunder.   A stray piece of wood
belonging to, and about to form the side of, a hut
was lawful prize,—if possible it would be abstracted,
tin cans, stray shirts put out to dry, nothing came
amiss to the omnipresent, ever active Zouave.   Occasionally they were caught in the very act of delinquency, and confined in the guard tents, but if the
men of the guard were not very watchful they were
certain to get away.   The only security was tying
them.

It was generally found these good humoured
bandits came from a long distance off, and necessarily
were absent from their regiments,—by us deemed a
serious delinquency.   If made prisoners they were
handed over to the nearest French corps, who then
passed them on by guard from regiment to regiment
until they reached their own.

Then again, a French soldier might be seen for
hours together asleep under a few stones or under a
wall.   No cognisance seemed to be taken of absence,

nor did the man's comrades appear to care what became of him. Drunkenness too is not the uncommon
vice supposed amongst the French soldiers. But then
the temperament of the natives of the two nations
must be considered. For whilst an English soldier gets
obstinately, furiously, or stupidly drunk, a Frenchman
merely gets convivially or cheerfully so, and often
have the guards for the French trenches been seen
marching down with several in their ranks disguised
by liquor. This seemed to be thought "a good joke,"
producing no further notice than peals of laughter,
in which the officers joined.

But it is fair to state that, amongst the French,
no single regiment of the Line is held in very high
military estimation as compared with the Zouaves,
the Chasseurs de Vincennes, the Legion Etrangère,
and the recently raised Guardes Imperial. All these
are composed of volunteers, tempted by various in-
ducements, who adopt the military life as their trade
or profession.

The first, after certain length of service, have
grants of land in Algeria made to them, and, when
not actively employed, can work at whatever labour
they select, never ceasing, however, to be soldiers.

I

The others have higher rates of pay, or some other strong temptation, but whatever the inducement may be, the men composing these regiments are soldiers and volunteers in their ranks by profession.

On the other hand, two-thirds of those filling the ranks of regiments of the French Line are conscripts drawn by ballot, looking to the moment when the time shall arrive for their release from the forced military servitude they are undergoing, and only held to the ranks by the severe penalties awaiting deserters.

It can be easily understood that, amongst the "Line regiments," the discipline being loose as regards the habits and conduct of the soldiers, the men held together temporarily (annually the term of the conscripts of a particular year expires), having no strong ties of love for their military duties. Commanded by officers in no respect their superiors in the social scale, but frequently the reverse, they are not prone to show the stubborn determination in attack, nor the fixed resolution to be victorious which characterise soldiers brought up to the profession of arms, accustomed to act together, and to look to their leader's orders and authority as the sole and undivided guide.

Such feelings are instilled only by strict and severe discipline, and by long service. They produce what is termed a soldier, and in no country in the world, nor in any age, has discipline been brought to a greater pitch than in the British army of to-day.

Our colonial possessions, by severing the ties of the individual in the ranks from friends and connections, identify them with their regiments, and thus promote unity of feeling, obedience, and action nowhere else to be found. A company of British soldiers, with from five to ten years' colonial service, is fit for any work—would obey any order with unflinching, unconquerable stubbornness which death alone could overcome. Of such men the army of the Alma was mostly composed, and time alone can replace and re-produce them.

When the discipline of the French army is described as habitually lax it must, however, be remembered that punishments in time of war for crimes which, with us, subject the delinquent to temporary corporeal suffering only, are, with our ally, punished with nothing less than death, and the sentence of death and its execution are carried out in an equally summary manner.

The result of the habitually lax discipline in trifles (here endeavoured to be described), leads, with the French, to serious crimes committed in cold blood, such crimes, indeed, as with the British rarely take place, and when they do occur the delinquent is sure to be found under the influence of liquor. Thus it has happened commonly that the French, even under fire in the trenches, have been careless, inattentive, or wilfully disobedient to orders, or still worse, have struck their superiors; on one occasion an offender, who had been guilty of the latter crime and struck an officer, was forthwith led out and shot in the middle ravine. Whether a court-martial or "conseil de guerre" had regularly assembled, recorded the proceedings, and awarded the punishment is uncertain, but probably the crime was committed in the presence of numbers, and three or four superior officers decided on the retribution.

Just when the patience of all was nearly exhausted rumour was again rife respecting an attack, and on this occasion there was some foundation. The men were ready to brave everything to alter the monotonous, tedious, and laborious trench duty.

Early in the forenoon of the 7th June orders were suddenly issued that officers and men were to be confined to camp, and about the same time long narrow close lines of French were seen marching from the south-east of the plateau in two columns, one towards the right or White House ravine, and the other along the hollow terminating and forming the middle ravine, and leading to the French works connecting the British right with the French left, as also to the covered way to Gordon's battery, the ordinary route for the English trench guard to relieve.

The sight was most singular. The two vast columns, perhaps twenty thousand each, seemed like long interminable lines of laborious ants. Shortly afterwards further divisional and brigade orders were issued, and we then became aware that the Quarries were the works which the British were destined to attack, whilst the French assaulted the Mamelon. As men fight far better on full than on empty stomachs, one day's cold provisions were ordered and prepared, and the officers, taking the hint that

possibly they might not see their camp for some
time, dined early, and carried away with them
a supply of cold food to guard against con-
tingencies.

The regiment to which we belonged was to give
one hundred men with a captain as an attacking
or storming party ; two hundred men were also
appointed as a working party, to secure our ground
as we advanced, and to throw up cover and form a
line of defence ; the other regiments of the brigade
were called on for parties of nearly the same strength,
some as supports, some as working parties, and some
for stormers.

The regiments belonging to the 2d Brigade of the
Light Division gave similar numbers, and the gallant
2d Division, the companion and brother of the Light
Division in hard work, in manning the trenches of
the right attack, in a word, in bearing the principal
portion of the hard knocks and labour connected
with the siege, supplied possibly a stronger force.
Then there were additional guards for the trenches,
and the remainders of the troops of the two divisions
were ordered to form up each in front of its respective
regimental camp, and there to remain.

This, as may readily be imagined, was no very agreeable position : too far off to tell exactly what was going on, but near enough to hear and see the fire without being able to ascertain the result except by gleaning intelligence from the vague, doubtful, and often contradictory rumours and tales brought by the wounded, who either struggled to the rear or were occasionally carried in.

The regiment, being formed in column, those next for duty were taken for the required service. This was much the fairest way. Had volunteering been permitted the whole of the men would have stepped out, ready to be employed, and the difficulty would then have been to select those who should remain. It is a painful task to refuse a request for permission to volunteer for perilous service. On this occasion a fine old sergeant—an invaluable man, because he was a soldier of sixteen years' service, whose bearing and example gave confidence to the young ones— begged to be permitted to take the place of another colour-sergeant whose company was named for the duty. Of course it was necessary to negative this request, for if it had been granted to one non-commissioned officer to exchange, in other words, to volunteer, such indulgence (inappropriate as this definition may seem), could not with justice have been refused to others.

To those who entirely disbelieve in premonishment, or rather to a species of fore-warning occasionally vouchsafed to individuals, it may be curious to state it transpired subsequently, that the colour-sergeant whom his comrade wished to supersede and to leave at home, was a man highly esteemed and respected ; he was, moreover, the son of a late adjutant, and was deservedly specially considered in the regiment. He had served very creditably at Alma, at Inkerman, and during the siege, but for weeks he had felt a presentiment his hour was near at hand, that death would shortly overtake him. He had closed his worldly concerns, sold many of his effects, sent letters giving away some valued trifles, and left clearly-written instructions as to the remainder. As a last resource his comrades desired to frustrate the fixed idea by leaving him (the colour-sergeant) behind, and filling his place with another sergeant. But this was not permitted. The presentiment was fulfilled; after being about half-an-hour in the attack he was literally knocked to pieces by a shell, and the remains of his corpse were brought into camp the next morning.

It is singular how frequently such presentiments are felt, how constantly they are realised. In this instance more than the ordinary passive and trying dangers of the trenches had been endured; there was at the time no certainty of attack, and only within a few hours of it had the regiment been ordered for special service; yet for days this poor fellow believed his course was nearly run, and even at last the kind endeavour of a comrade to reassure and change the impression on his mind by taking his place had been disappointed.

In recording this fact it is only right to add, presentiments of death felt and acknowledged have often turned out incorrect; it is equally certain that most men who think about the matter previously to action write some memoranda, and if they fall, it is often without reason alleged they knew they were to die; but the fact is, they merely acted as the majority of prudent and brave men, if time permit, are disposed to do. Still in this case there was a settled conviction, only exceeded by that of a brigadier, who unfortunately was killed on the succeeding 18th of June.

About half-past five the English force intended for the' Quarries marched down, and at half-past six the attack began by the French successfully taking possession of the Mamelon. They suddenly appeared, rapidly advanced in force, and were soon in the works, the enemy flying in all directions, abandoning guns, arms, and ammunition, concentrating all their energies upon securing their individual safety.

The advanced, or attacking parties, were followed by dense columns of supports. Quickly everything was wrapped in smoke, and, with the exception of the French columns, the Mamelon was seen only at intervals. Suddenly, in one of these, a French column, already partially in possession of the enemy's works, was seen to waver, hesitate, break, and finally crowds were running down the Mamelon, threatening to sweep clear away an advancing battalion of Zouaves. Fortunately they did not do so, as the latter stood firm, and happily no harm was done.

Success had evidently attended the columns on the right, for, carried away by their own impetuosity, they not only gained the post intended to be assailed, but went long past it; stragglers were observed close up to and on the glacis of the Malakoff, and a hot contest raged immediately up to the work. Some of these driven back long beyond the Mamelon, from the fruitless struggles which they gratuitously undertook, caused the panic which threatened for a moment to be fatal to one of the most important enterprises of the whole war.

But the French, amidst a most tremendous fire, held their own,—they remained masters of the Mamelon, which, once in possession of the Allies, gave the first dim promise of success to the siege. The French commander-in-chief stationed himself in the remains of what was originally termed "The Five-Gun Battery." It was just in front, about fifty yards below the Victoria Redoubt, an admirable spot to view the French attack, and affording a fair view of part of the British right attack.

Meanwhile, along the valley to the left of the French, long and continued musketry fire was heard, mingled with cheering, but the whole was enveloped in such dense smoke, with night falling, that nothing could be seen. This noise was caused by the

British overcoming the three Russian lines of defence
(of "attack" would be an equally appropriate term,
the enemy having regularly conducted their approaches in the shape of a few apparently insignificant rifle pits, and then connecting them together
until we became, as it were, the besieged), and gain-
ing the Quarries.

To turn these lines of defence and make them
serve as our own was the object of the workers, but
so desperate and so often repeated were the Russian
endeavours to regain ground lost, that many of the
working parties assisted as a guard to enable us to
hold our position.

We, too, like our allies, were partially carried
away by impetuosity. The gallant 88th suffered
considerably from this cause.

From about eight o'clock wounded Frenchmen had
been continually passing our camp, and dropping in
from the front, but no reliable information could be
gained from them. Most of the slightly hurt were
more or less excited and unable to give any connected
account except of their own acts and deeds, of which
there was profuse mention; some, indeed, appeared
so much elated as to be out of their ordinary senses.

Prisoners also now began to be brought in.   Poor, miserable,   half-starved   creatures   they   appeared. These gave us hope, and about ten o'clock it was proclaimed that everywhere success had attended the Allied attack.   The French not only remained mas- ters of the Mamelon, but also carried and kept the White Buildings, where they had been unsuccessful in their attack in the preceding February ; whilst the British overcame the three formidable Russian paral- lels, and seized the Quarries.

About fifty-six thousand men were engaged in the first named enterprise,—scarcely four thousand in the last.   The Allies having successfully carried the posi- tions for which they fought, the difficulty now was to hold them securely.

After we had taken possession of the Quarries the enemy was continually harassing us in one form or another, but so little success attended their efforts that their soldiers all but refused the duty.   In one of these attacks a non-commissioned officer of the 47th heroically distinguished himself.   In the early days of June an officer had succeeded in getting four of his men to approach our works.   They quickly caught the eye of lance-corporal Quin, who, without the least hesitation, rifle in hand and unaided, rushed on the five, settled one with his bayonet, floored a second with the butt of his rifle, and did it in less time than we take to tell it. The other two privates ran for dear life, and the officer and Quin were left face to face. Quin seized his prisoner, made him march before him into the works, and delivered him over to the officer in command. Such deeds show the character of the true English soldier.

We passed through the night of the 7th and morning of the 8th most anxiously. It was a nervous time. The heavy firing of musketry at intervals showed that repeated and sharp assaults were continued. At length the welcome daylight proved that we now possessed the works which had grown up under our very eyes; works which, commencing perhaps with a single rifle pit, gradually increased until they became most formidable for defence, and which paucity of material, sickness, and the small number of men rendered us too feeble to attempt to prevent or interrupt.

And when the common question arises, why did not the British establish solid roads from Balaclava to the front immediately after the commencement of the siege in October 1854 ? it must always be remembered that perhaps no army in the world, with such totally inadequate numbers, and with such suffering and sickness, ever successfully held such an extended line of operations as the British army before Sebastopol during the winter 1854-5.

The French army, which had been on the right, and had the advantage of the sea line on its flank after landing in the Crimea and on the advance to the Alma, shortly after the Allied forces came before Sebastopol took the left, again had the sea, and enjoyed of course the same advantages. Not until late in February did the French come in any considerable strength to aid in diminishing our too extended lines ; after their army was augmented they took the right, and then we were in the centre.

On Saturday the 9th of June, at twelve o'clock, a truce was proclaimed. At first it was supposed the line of flags would merely stand an hour for the purpose of bringing in and burying the dead ; but gradually the time was prolonged by an hour, half-an-hour, and so continued until it was past five before they were struck.

During the truce many visited the interior of that

extraordinary work, "The Mamelon Verte;" others
went to look for friends or comrades who had fallen.
Our enemy availed themselves of the prolonged truce
to haul out two ships from Careening Bay, and it is
supposed were mounting fresh guns on their works.

We, too, were not idle, but were busily occupied in
strengthening part of our lines. The allies believed
the Russians lengthened out the original period
assigned for the truce mainly for the purpose of
hauling out their ships, and newly arming some of
their works. The Russians attributed similar motives
to the Allies. On the other hand it was said that the
latter availed themselves of this valuable time only
when they perceived what the enemy was about.
The truth of the matter will probably never be
known, but the belief of the Allies was strengthened
by the fact, that the moment the truce was ended a
heavy cannonade was opened by the Russians along
their whole line. The time chosen for this was
unusual also; it was just when our reliefs were
taking place, and although they must have known
previously by spies and must have seen the French
guards relieving, they had usually refrained from
annoying us up to this time. Whether the ships

were hauled out during the truce or previously, we cannot positively say, but the ships' guns were immediately brought to bear on the French and caused a good deal of mischief in the Mamelon.

During the truce the sappers (and many others for amusement) examined the ground for "fougasses." In this employment all trod carefully. It was quite extraordinary that so few exploded on the 7th of June, for more than one hundred were dug up and taken away from that part of the right attack between Egerton Pit and the Quarries ; over this space some thousands of feet must have passed, yet on this occasion only one or two blew up, and only one that gave rise to much conversation, the case of Captain Armstrong, 49th Regiment. He was wounded early, placed on a stretcher, and was being carried off by four men, a fifth and sixth following, when one of his bearers, treading on a fougasse, the Captain and the whole party were blown up. His hands, which were hanging outside the stretcher on each side, were sadly scorched, and the men were more or less severely injured, yet fortunately no life was lost ; after a long detention in hospital all ultimately recovered.

K

The fougasse is a square or oblong case, made of metal or stout timber bound with iron hoops; in either case it is filled with gunpowder or gunpowder enclosed in bottles, grenades, or shells, or a mixture of both, or all three. The case itself is buried from an inch to a foot below the soil. Gutta-percha or other pipes, filled with gunpowder, spring from each end; these rise above the surface, and are connected together by a few inches of glass tubing, containing at one end some phosphoric preparation, and at the other a few drops of powerful acid, or perhaps altogether loaded with detonating powder. This glass tube, when broken either by the foot getting entangled in it, or by the direct pressure of the foot, ignites the charge, and an unexpected mine is fired.

It frequently happened that on the space where hundreds of men had been in the daily habit of passing, some of these infernal weapons were dis-covered, and the actual explosion did not inflict such injury as the dread engendered amongst the men by these diabolical, hidden, machines; the very feeling which the enemy was naturally anxious to cause. If a fougasse to destroy a few could be constructed or rather arranged so ingeniously, why should not similar contrivances on a large scale exist? was the argument.

The ignition of a fougasse at night on the 11th of June did not fail to increase this feeling of hidden danger. It was seen to perfection by nearly a thousand men or more, amid the cries and screams of the injured, and most eye-witnesses secretly felt certain a fougasse had exploded, though publicly it was attributed to carelessness in conveying powder.

On this night it happened the Second Division gave the party to hold our new acquisition of the Quarries, and the supports of this part of the trench guard were formed by the Light Division, which was located in, and to the right and left in rear of, Egerton's Pit, and the Pit itself was the head-quarters of the support. Barrels of small arm ammunition were brought here so as to be close at hand if the party in the Quarries ran short.

On the British side during the night, excepting shelling, we were tolerably silent, the artillery being engaged in conveying guns across the open from the right to arm the Quarries, whilst large working parties of the line were employed both in carrying material by a similar route, and in taking ammunition through the trenches.

The firing of the enemy had been occasional, coming at unexpected moments, but was not heavy or continuous. Whilst passing the dark hours (for there was little moon) we were much excited by seeing a considerable explosion, followed immediately by English cries and screams. Of course these only lasted for a moment, the enemy instantly opening fire on the spot so unluckily pointed out. As before stated, most of us in our hearts guessed the true cause of the explosion, yet we endeavoured to cheat the men into the belief it was merely a barrel of powder ignited through carelessness.

It subsequently turned out that one of the working parties, consisting of about three hundred men under the command of Major Herbert of the 23d Regiment, was proceeding from the right across the open towards the Quarries, and it is certain that the whole detachment, straggling in their progress over the ground in line about a couple of hundred yards in length, and perhaps seven or eight feet in breadth, must have passed over where the fougasse was buried, yet stranger still to say, it was only one of the rear men, carrying the stretcher (for no party moved without a stretcher) that had the misfortune to break the tube and cause the explosion. Three men were killed on the spot and many more were wounded; the major himself having a narrow escape, being covered with blood, and the debris of the killed. The loss itself was nothing compared to the moral depression it raised amongst the division, and those who witnessed the sight.

The fire of the enemy immediately directed to the spot proved harmless.

CHAPTER IX.

THE practice of the mortars on the night of the 11th
of June was the most regular that had been yet
seen, or that the Russians had experienced. The
batteries of both the right and left attacks acted
together in perfect confederation ; no sooner had the
shelling from one battery ceased, than it was taken
up in succession by the others. It must have been
productive of considerable damage, for shells falling

beyond the Redan still created mischief amongst the enemy in the rear of it.

The sight was most picturesque and interesting, for the path of a shell through the air was clearly seen by means of its fuse, and speculation employed itself in guessing whether the missile would burst within or beyond the Redan. Occasionally no doubt was left as to the effect, the glare and explosion showing dark pieces of mortality thrown up.

Shortly after midnight the shelling ceased, and hardly had it so done when a rattling of musketry commenced. Nobody exactly knew the cause, but there was a gradual inclination to our flank (the left of our right attack), where the Woronzoff road runs between two cliffs, one being the boundary of the right British attack, the other, the right of the left British attack.

All stood to their arms. The night was very dark, and there was an idea prevalent that the Russians would endeavour cautiously to creep round, and take the Quarries in reverse. Fortunately the origin of the alarm was trifling. A working party on the side of the left attack had allowed a gabion to get loose, and this, rolling down the precipitous bank into the road, had made some noise, and created the alarm which we were glad to find was nothing more serious. Afterwards, everything went on tranquilly until dawn, when some heavy firing from the enemy took place, and a shell, bursting in Egerton's Pit, blew up the few barrels of reserve small arm ammunition therein recently deposited, at the same time killing or injuring about half-a-dozen men.

Late on the evening of the 15th June, Sir George Brown returned fresh and elated from the Kertch expedition, and on the following day resumed command of the remains of the Light Division, but his command was temporary. On the 17th (Sunday) he was appointed to take charge of, and to superintend the contemplated attack on, the Redan.

That unfortunate undertaking was arranged to take place on the anniversary of the 18th June 1815, in order to cement the cordial alliance now existing between the two chief adversaries of that day, and so, by the conclusion of this ever memorable siege, render it still more famous by substituting for the future " Sebastopol " for " Waterloo."

At 4 A.M. our fire opened briskly and continued until twelve, when there was a lull. The Malakoff answered feebly, and the small battery on its right appeared to be silenced by the fire from the Quarries.

In the evening the orders, placing Sir George Brown in command of the attack, were issued. This caused the senior brigadier (Codrington) to fall into the command of the division, and the senior colonel (Yea) of the brigade. The latter was also to conduct the attack on the left face of the Redan. Covering parties of the rifles were to go out from the works near the Quarries, where the storming or attacking party of volunteers from the 23d Regiment, under Colonel Lysons, were intended to be formed, whilst the 7th, 33d, and 34th Regiments were to be in support and placed in the Boyaus and covered way on the right of the right attack which connected us with the French.

These supports, as soon as the attack commenced, were to proceed across the open and thus approach the stormers. We were to move off from our camps punctually at 11.30 P.M., and to remain in the trenches until a signal should be sent up from that part of our works termed the 8-gun battery. In the meantime it was understood that previously to the signal for attack being made, our guns should be employed in playing on the abattis of the Redan, and destroying it. Upon the cessation of fire, and the signal arranged, the covering party of the rifles was to open, a company of the rifle brigade was detailed as the wool-bag party with these necessary materials to fill the ditch, the sailors under Captain Peel with ladders, and the stormers were to sally forth from a spot adjacent to the Quarries; as soon as fairly launched, as before observed, the supports were to issue from the right and advance across the open—a distance said to be 800 yards, but really nearer 1200, on the left face of the Redan.

Such was the plan.* All knew their work, were prepared and acquainted with the respective localities

*Division Orders, 17th June 1855.

1. The Light Division being about to be employed with others in the attack on the Redan, provisions will be issued and cooked for to-morrow, and care must be taken that the men's canteens are filled with water this afternoon. Each man will be provided with twenty rounds additional ammunition to be carried in his haversack.

2. The whole guard of the trenches will be furnished this evening from the 2d brigade, and that portion of the brigade which is not so employed will be formed in the morning in the first parallel to the right of the 21-gun battery, where it will be joined by the reserve of the trenches at daylight.

3. Weakly men and recruits will be selected for the camp guard and the general care of the camp, where they are to remain, and will be directed not to show themselves on the high ground in front.

4. The lieutenant-general having been charged with three columns of attack, the command of the light division will for the moment devolve on Major-General Codrington.

from which they were to act. And as volunteers are said to be "worth double the number of pressed

5. The officer in command of the guards of the trenches will take care to make such a disposition of his men as shall leave room for the additional troops which it is proposed shall be sent forward to the attack.

6. The right attack will be made by the 1st brigade under Colonel Yea, 7th Royal Fusiliers, in the following order :—

First, 100 men of the rifle brigade as a covering party ; next, 50 men with wool sacks, to be furnished by the rifle brigade ; next 400 men of the 23d and 34th under Lieutenant-Colonel Lysons, 23d Royal Welch Fusiliers, together with the sappers and seamen carrying ladders, to be formed in the Quarries and in the two Russian trenches on the right of them which have been appropriated, leaving room on the left for a detachment of the same strength from the 4th division, and the support which will consist of 800 men.

From the 7th, 33d, and 34th regiments.

These will be immediately followed by the working party consisting of 200 men of the Rifle Brigade, 100 of the 23d Fusiliers, and 100 of the 34th regiment.

7. The utmost silence must be maintained on proceeding to the trenches, and after the troops shall have arrived there, and care must be taken that until the assault shall be ordered to take place, no man is to be allowed to show his head above the parapet.

BRIGADE ORDERS, 17th June 1855.

For the attack on the Redan to-morrow morning, the following will be the detail :—

The Rifle Brigade will furnish 200 men for a covering party to keep down the fire of the batteries, 110 men for carrying ladders and wool packs, under the command of Major Macdonnell.

The 23d will furnish 200 men under Lieutenant-Colonel Lysons, and the 34th 200, under Captain Guilt, to form the attacking party, the whole under the command of Lieutenant-Colonel Lysons.

The support will consist of 7th and 33d regiments, with 200 of the 34th regiment.

men," considerable confidence was felt by the circumstance that Colonel Lysons, with picked volunteers
from his own regiment and the 34th, were to be the
stormers.

We had been busy serving out a day's provisions,
and after some few hours' rest were about to fall in,
when the programme was suddenly changed. The
foundation of the arrangement was altered. The 23d
under Colonel Lysons was not to form part of the
storming party, but to join the 7th and 33d and be the
supports, whilst the 34th alone was to act in the first
capacity. This change caused some delay, but about
a quarter to twelve we moved off to the rendezvous.

The working party will consist of 200 men of the Rifles, 100 of the
34th, and 100 of the 23d, under the command of Major Herbert, 23d.

The whole will be formed right in front at the rendezvous of the
right division at half past twelve to-night.

The covering party will be on the right, the attacking party next to
them, and the support following.

The covering party and the attacking party will occupy the parallel
and the pits on the right of the Quarries, the support will occupy the
two Boyaus in the right front of the old advance.

The 110 men forming the ladder and wool pack party will proceed
to the engineering store on the right of the Lancaster Battery.

The 400 men of a working party, under Major Herbert, will proceed
to the same spot, and will have their position pointed out to them by
an officer of engineers.

The residue of the regiments of the brigade will be formed as a
reserve in the first parallel and will be attached to the 2d brigade.

At the same time heavy columns of French were also coming down towards the entrance of the Middle Ravine, in order to cross the spit of land terminating in the Victoria Redoubt, and in front of the encampment of the 1st brigade, and so in the attack on the Malakoff to join the troops concentrated in the right ravine, on the other or eastern side of the said spit.

The night was dark, and it was difficult, until quite close, to distinguish troops which were near at hand—this seemingly interminable column was cross- ing the front of ours, but, waiting patiently until an opening occurred, on we pushed, crossing the re- mainder of the French, ascended the opposite side of the ravine, and then were fairly *en route.*

On arrival at the spot which used to be the rendezvous for the guards going on duty in the trenches, we found the 34th drawn up silently in column, with the lamented Yea in waiting to explain our further movements. The 34th was directed to incline to the left, and then to defile through the trenches to the spot whence they were to issue for the attack. Our column, composed of the greater part of the 7th, 33d, and 23d Regiments in their order of for- mation, as written, proceeded straight to its front until it reached the 21-gun battery, then across the open and filed to its destined position.

This position was most excellent for observation. The column was directly in front, the right hand man of the leading Regiment, the 7th, being at the extremity of one of the Boyaus, which ran out nearly at right angles with the covered way connecting us with the French, and nearly parallel with our own old advance work.

Thus on standing to our arms we had our faces to the latter, and on the word being given the formation was simple.   There was nothing further to do than, by divisions, to bring our left shoulders forward ; we were in open columns of companies, the pivot flank being thus towards our own works, the reverse flank towards the Russians, we could advance without the smallest confusion.   Thus, too, as we rested and waited in the trenches we could see what was going on in our own defences, and had the most favourable spot for seeing the French attack, for the Malakoff was in full view, and the formidable left face of the Redan seemed as if its guns could enfilade us.

As we marched down there was an ominous still-ness, in fact literally there was no firing.   The solitary report of a gun would have been a relief—it would have shown things were much as usual, but the unwonted silence made it appear that the enemy was aware of what was about to take place, and was bent on allowing us full scope for our enterprise. During the armistice subsequent to the siege Russian officers stated that, in Sebastopol, they were thoroughly acquainted with our movements.

The weather had been hot, and old tents and canvass had been issued to use as sun screens for those on duty in the trenches, and they were so used by each successive guard.   Plentifully scattered everywhere, they now proved admirably adapted as couches to keep us off the ground.   Many men here reclined for their last repose, whilst others smoked or chatted heedless or ignorant of the next day's struggle, or rather, of the next day's passive endurance of the enemy's iron storm.

As dawn approached it became known that the guns were not to open, and that, instead of our waiting for the signal to attack after two hours' bombardment, we were to look for it shortly after the French assault on the Malakoff.   The Brigadier (Yea) came across from the Quarries and took post at the extremity of the Boyaus, that he might there watch for the commencement of the action.

The day had hardly broken when a rocket was sent up from some spot near the Victoria Redoubt; this was answered by another from the Mamelon, and then there was a general movement amongst us, thinking one of these was the agreed signal or the precursor of it.   Almost at the very moment a small dark flag was hoisted at the Malakoff, and, amidst a tremendous fire, our allies in crowds were seen on the glacis of the Malakoff, where every sort of fougasse, mine, and combustible seemed exploding; then a cessation of fire, and then a recommencement, and then again everything was hidden from view except flashes and smoke on the Malakoff side.

Whilst watching the Malakoff, probably a few minutes, the Rifles stationed close to the Quarries as a covering party, having evidently mistaken one of the French rockets for the British signal, commenced firing from their hiding-places, when round shot dropping about from the Redan, proved our red jackets were observed.   The error of the coverers was great and considerably annoyed the Brigadier, who, pointing to a flagstaff near the 8-gun battery,

said, "A flag will be hoisted there where Lord
Raglan stands." He added, "That fire (alluding to
the covering party of the Rifles) must be stopped.
Somebody must go across the open; it is no use
attempting to get through the trenches."

Moments like these try the mettle of men, and
prove of what they are made. No mere bravado
answers, for that always fails when actual and
perilous deeds of cool and deliberate courage have to
be performed. Whoever volunteered to fulfil the
Brigadier's mission knew he must go as it were with
his life in his hand. Not only every step, but every
inch of the distance between the trenches and the
covering party was strewn with peril, and carrying
the message and escaping with life was not for an
instant to be looked for.

A momentary silence ensued. The fire from all
arms was pounding away in every direction, and the
service was very periculous. To cross the open and
reach the Quarries we saw and knew exposure to the
fire from the Malakhof was certain, and the able
marksmen and the guns of the Redan* were also to
be encountered. The duty was seen to be so

* The left face.

momentous that all hesitated to undertake it, not from fear, but from the feeling of all but certain failure. Brigadier Yea then repeated his desire, saying, "Who will go?" Then there was another pause, when every soldier who heard his leader's request felt his heart beat with intense rapidity, and every mental energy of his mind awakened. For a few moments there was intense silence amongst us, and then quickly and nervously Captain Cooper, one of his aides-de-camp, answered, " I will, Sir." And out this gallant officer went.

Springing over the trench, commencing with a quick walk, he increased his pace gradually till he ran. His eyes were fixed upon the Rifles, all eyes were upon him. All expected to see him fall, but Providence guarded him. He reached the Quarries, and stopped the fire, his life most probably preserved by this courageous act of gallantry, for the crowd and confusion at the opening of the miserably small trench whence the stormers issued were so great, he never could have rejoined his lamented chief had he gone by the way of the trenches.

Yet, though many an officer and many a man have received the Victoria Cross for the common act of humanity *—aiding or assisting to bring in a wounded officer, or comrade, under circumstances of danger,— acts which most of us at the time they happened thought little about, and certainly never regarded them as deserving the designation of "distinguished," —*for the above gallant act, setting an example of the highest devotion to the service of his Queen and country in the face of hundreds, this officer received no reward.*

Hardly had the sharp-shooters' fire been arrested when the signal was given to advance. It was as nearly as possible half-past three in the morning of the 18th of June. Colonel Lysons, commanding the column of supports, gave the command. The man-œuvre, as before noted, was simple : as soon as

---

* Acts, thought little of at the time, indeed often remaining unnoticed, such as aiding, assisting, or being instrumental in assisting or bringing in wounded became common, but after the war these were, if it may be so expressed, "dug up," and many a man, to his own surprise, certainly to the astonishment of survivors, figured in the *London Gazette* as a recipient of the Victoria Cross. Whether the *lavish* bestowal of this distinction for assisting the wounded at the siege may not hereafter tend to encourage breach of the sixty-fourth Article of War remains to be seen—it says :—" who shall leave the ranks in order to secure prisoners, or horses, or on pretence of taking wounded officers or men to the rear, without orders from his superior officer, or——." Unfortunately experience proves that volunteers are rarely wanting to assist the wounded, and under this plea to quit the field.

the divisions brought their left shoulders square we advanced in open columns of companies, the 7th Fusiliers leading, under the command of its major.

The first two companies had gone about fifty yards only into the open space when it became obvious, under such a fire as was then being discharged from the enemy's batteries, no troops could possibly live. The fire was fierce from the left face of the Redan, and also from the Malakoff.   By this time their defenders had found they had not much to fear from the French; they were therefore enabled to devote their attention almost wholly to the British, and from our flag, they imagined most probably to Lord Raglan's party, as well as to the column marching in front of the works exposed to the deadly cross fire of the two forts.

When soldiers are under heavy fire, like the rest of the world, they are glad to get out of it in the best way they can.   The leading companies of the Fusiliers were about to advance at the "double," * but they were quickly checked; our leader Colonel Lysons, as if on parade, stopped them, and only after

* The military run.

steadying the column, when it was thoroughly formed, would he allow it to advance at this desirable pace.

The Brigadier, observing the state of affairs, went back a short distance for the purpose, it is supposed, of communicating with Sir George Brown or General Codrington, who were looking on from the trench, and saying audibly, "it is too late," he, with his bugler, his orderly sergeant, and his remaining * aide-de-camp, ran with the column. The bugler was wounded very quickly, the orderly sergeant and aide-de-camp, running in file, were struck by grape, probably by the same ball, for they were both hit just below the hip on the left side. The sergeant, after recovering the numbness of his wound in the friendly shelter afforded by the crater of an exploded shell, was killed in endeavouring to get home, whilst the aide-de-camp, having more patiently waited the course of events in a similar asylum, succeeded in reaching his camp with a severe wound, but no bones broken.

Brigadier Yea was thus left alone, and the exact moment of his fate is uncertain, for, after being

* Lord Richard Brown.

wounded, he was shot through the back part of the head, and fell close to the abatis of the Redan.

We cannot part from Brigadier Yea without again referring to the accepted (by many) theory of pre-monishment, of which he would appear to be an example. Soldiers engaged in active warfare, in the excitement and daily perils of their life, do not usually dwell on the certainty of dying on the battlefield or in the trenches ; on the contrary, such is the buoyancy of the human mind, they rather calculate on the chances of escape, or at least with escape possibly wounded, and they shelve and put away from all contemplation, generally, the subject of death. Escape to-day increases faith in the certainty of escape to-morrow, and so the soldier pursues his duty as steadily and fully and often more thoughtlessly than the mechanic pursues his daily avocations.

But to this there are many exceptions. Nervous temperaments engaged in war are irresistibly drawn to believe that they will die in the conflict some day, but that they will eventually escape they will not believe. And yet those who thus believe in their irrevocable fall often pass through all the events of a campaign, engaged in the fiercest of the actions, and return to their homes, in many cases, without a wound.

Such cases do not come within the province of what is termed " premonishment." By this is meant, that some psychological causes are put into operation bearing into the mind of the individual concerned, silent but certain intuitive warnings that his days are numbered. What those causes are, and whence they derive their knowledge, or whether it is not a gracious warning from a divine origin to prepare the soul for its departure we cannot tell, but that such intuitions have been given, have been received as such, have been acted upon, and have been fulfilled it is useless to deny.

Brigadier Yea had been actively engaged in the Crimea from the first—he held an important command in the battle of the Alma, also in the battle of Inkerman—he was an able, vigilant, and careful soldier, held in high esteem by his superiors, possessing the confidence of his men. Plain and straightforward there was no claim or pretension on his part to be what is termed a religious man. The plans for the attack on the Redan were all arranged by Sunday, the 17th of June. Having made his will, wherein he left his little cob on which he rode in the battles of Alma and Inkerman to Captain Goodlake of the Guards, and his charger to Lord Vivian of Glyn, and a legacy of five pounds to his soldier-servant George Smith, he partook of the Holy Communion in the hut at the close of divine service, apparently deeply impressed.

Early on Monday morning, Smith, with his cob, was waiting for his master. On his arrival the Brigadier's first words were, " Smith, they have dis-arranged all the plans previously agreed upon," and after a sentence or two more, " he took me by the hand"—this he had *never* previously done—and shaking it, said, " Good-bye, Smith, take care of yourself—if I fall, keep close to me," and then started for the scene of action. His manner clearly showed his conviction that his end was near, and, like a good soldier as he was, he was bracing himself for the fight. He had just passed the second parapet looking towards the Redan, when the shot struck him and he fell dead on the spot.

Being the senior major, the command of the 7th Fusiliers now devolved upon us. Scarcely had we assumed the direction of the regiment, when a ball from a minie rifle passed fiercely right through the fleshy part of our left leg cutting a round hole in the thick cloth of the trousers on entering, and also another on leaving, and we were at once placed hors de combat, and compelled to retire from the attack. As soldiers usually say, " every bullet has its billet."

The history of the unfortunate column is pretty well known. It successively crossed the three Russian lines or parallels taken by us on the 7th of June, and arrived close to the abatis bordering the ditch of the Redan. This it did before the whole of the storming party could issue from their appointed narrow opening near the Quarries; all was in confusion, the jack-tars with the ladders scattered, the wool-sacks lying about, and a formidable unbroken abatis in front—the column gradually edged to the left, and entered the distant trenches near the Quarries as best it could.

As has been stated, no troops could live under such a fire. The weather, having been very dry, the ground was so parched that the missiles, as they struck, made the dust rise from the spot in clouds, and it is no exaggeration to compare this tremendous storm of shot and shell to a heavy downpour of rain falling on water ; advancing as we did, it was matter of astonishment that any succeeded in arriving unhurt at the abatis.

On each side of the embrasures of the left face of the Redan the enemy was standing up on the parapets in such crowds as apparently to hinder one another ; doubtless within the work others were actively engaged loading and handing up arms, so that, in our advance, we were destroyed or placed hors-de-combat as expeditiously as possible.

On our right was a small gully or ditch. Here many of the wounded, not liking to turn their backs to the Russians and go to the rear, edged off, and reached what seemed tolerably safe cover. Alas ! this safety was a delusion, for the ditch lay in a direct line with an embrasure on the left face of the Redan, and completely enfiladed by it ; no sooner did the wounded red jackets (for we were all dressed in red on this day, the weather being fine, and the grey colour of the great coat having caused mistakes before) congregate in numbers, than, for their especial benefit, a deadly fire was directed upon them from the Redan.

Then might be seen the slightly wounded endeavouring to get out, careless where they trod, whether on the maimed, on the dying, or on the dead, and then themselves shot, toppled over and fell across their comrades. Then were rifles, red jackets, and artillery (for a party of volunteers of the latter had accompanied and followed the stormers to spike the enemy's guns), all intermixed in every stage of misery, a living and dying mass of confusion where every round claimed fresh victims.

The yells and groans of the battle-field have been represented as horrible ; but it is more natural to believe that these yells and groans are subsequent to, and some time after, an action, where circumstances have prevented for a few hours the removal of the sufferers from the field. At all events, on this occasion there were scarcely any noises of this description. If a poor wounded man received a second hurt, or was mortally wounded he perhaps gave a cry, or breathed away life in a groan, but these were exceptions. Amongst the generality complete silence prevailed.

The fact is, a gun-shot wound (and these were all such), gives little or no pain at the first moment.

There is a deadened, paralysed feeling of the part which incapacitates from moving, or if a bone be broken, the human, like a hare or any other animal when shot, frequently only finds out the extent of the mischief when attempting to rise or to walk.

The losses to the columns of supports on this disastrous day were severe, but the portion of the 23d, which formed a part of it, being the rear regiment, was fortunately prevented by Sir George Brown, or by General Codrington, from uselessly going out of the trenches when it was seen the terrible gauntlet of fire the battalions encountered. Of these battalions the 7th, out of sixteen officers, five only escaped unhurt, and something like eighty-nine casualties happened to the men. The commanding officer of the 33d Regiment lost a hand before he had advanced ten yards, and his regiment suffered pretty equally. The major of the 7th (commanding) was brought in wounded from the Quarries; Colonel Lysons, the commander of the column, was also wounded. The acting Brigadier in charge of the attack on the left face, the gallant Yea, was killed close to the abatis ; here, too, fell Forman of the Rifle Brigade, shot in the stomach whilst

tying up the wound of his subaltern; young Hurst
of the 34th, supposed to be blown up by a fougasse, perished at this spot, and there lay the
bodies of Shiffner and Robinson of the same corps,
with many others.

In fact there are few actions of modern times
in which the proportions of casualties have been so
great, and the number of officers who fell, as compared with the men, so considerable. The abatis,
as it stood unbroken by our fire, was insurmount-
able, and besides, in the tempting openings left, the
deadly fougasse was abundantly planted.

As before stated, Lord Raglan was placed to view
the attack close to the gun battery. Who selected
the spot and posted his lordship near where his flag
was placed, and where his staff and the chief engineer Sir John Jones were assembled, is unknown;
but most of those stupid and dull infantry officers
who were not on the staff, but were conversant
with the locality (having probably for some months
daily and nightly spent at least twenty-four out of
every ninety-six hours in its vicinity), were well
aware that, for fifty yards to the eastward from the
angle where the bomb-proof called " The General's

Hut " was situated, at the descent from the above battery, was perhaps the most dangerous part of the trenches of the right attack, so much so that only an occasional sentry was posted—it was rarely lined by men, for it could be enfiladed by sharpshooters, and was fronting and in the direct line of the Malakoff guns.

Yet in this most dangerous spot Lord Raglan was placed, when he could have seen the attack fully as well, if not better, from Gordon's (the 21-gun) battery. Repeatedly was his lordship told of the danger of the position, but no notice was taken ; Colonel Shirley (88th) and several others suggested a change, but those advisers who had selected the spot would not yield. It was only when a round shot, striking the parapet, caused a stone to knock over the chief engineer,* and another striking nearly at the same instant, bounded over our parapet and killed a couple of men, besides taking off the arm of Captain Brown, 88th Regiment, that it was seen there was good reason for the suggestions.

Such arguments, ocular and convincing, were immediate in their solid effects, and our valued chief,

* Sir John Jones.

with those about him, moved up to the 21-gun battery. Thence Lord Raglan witnessed with grief the devastation caused by the enemy in our portion of the attack, and his lordship was to hear later the sad losses sustained by us on the other flank of the celebrated Redan.

Literal and absolute destruction had seemed to threaten all concerned in the attack on the left face of the Redan by the observers in the trenches, when Colonel Collingwood Dickson, who, at this time, commanded the Siege Train Royal Artillery of the right attack, seeing our utter failure, and the swarms of the enemy on the parapet and its embrasures deliberately shooting us down, went to Lord Raglan and begged permission to open fire; his lordship answered, "You will hurt our own people." The colonel, not deterred from his object, said, "I will stake my life on not doing so," and, without awaiting further instructions or seeking other orders, he caused guns and mortars to open. To this we attribute the fact that our losses were not greater than was actually the case, and that the wounded were pretty well got in.

From seven in the morning to half past four in the

afternoon parties came dropping into camp, and each had his own story to tell.

Then, during this time, the doctor and his assistants were in camp, with shirt sleeves tucked up, ready to attend, probe or cut as circumstances might require.

The common process was this : the moment the patient arrived to place the stretcher on the ground, examine the hurt, and probe it ; if a more serious operation were required, to order the wounded man to be thoroughly stripped preparatory to further proceedings. If, though severe, no bones were broken, the patient was put to bed, and lint or linen soaked in spring water was applied ; then, if a man were come to his full strength, of good constitution and healthy, the hurt soon began to show symptoms of healing. But if elderly the process was slower ; or if young, as many were— mere lads—possibly the youth succumbed to an injury which, to a grown man, might ultimately have been harmless.

Lieutenant-General Sir George Brown, harsh though he seemed in his general demeanour, was at heart a truly kind man. On the afternoon of the 18th, although at the time ill at ease, labouring under an attack of incipient cholera, and mentally bowed down with grief at the losses sustained and the unsuccessful result of the day, of which the most sanguine expectations had been entertained — for so great had been the confidence of our leaders that, previous to the attack, orders had been issued against marauding, and cavalry were brought to the front from Kadikoi forming a line of videttes to prevent the descent of camp followers to rob and pillage when the anticipated success should have crowned our efforts—Sir George visited most of the wounded officers and the regimental hospitals. To all he tried to say something kind, something to soothe the bitter feelings of pain and sorrow for the unfortunate failure.

Not many hours after he himself, having concealed the extent of his malady from even his immediate followers and staff, attempting to bear up against it, suddenly fainted after dinner, and was the next day taken down to Kamiesch and placed on board a steamer.

There he lingered between life and death for

M

several days, and at length sailed for England ; but Sir George was detained at Kamiesch long enough to learn the loss the country had sustained by the sudden demise of his patron, benefactor, and friend Lord Raglan. Major-General Codrington, too, weakened by exposure and anxieties, also sought repose and restoration on board ship, and went to Kamiesch for the benefit of his health ; the command of the Light Division thus temporarily devolved on the sturdy, never-failing, gallant Colonel Shirley of the 88th Regiment, the last surviving commanding officer of a regiment belonging to the Light Division who had landed in the Crimea * in September 1854, at the head of a regiment, and still continued so. Saunders of the 19th was ill from wounds ; Egerton of the 77th had been killed, Chester of the 23d fell at the Alma, Blake of the 33d had succumbed to the hardships he had suffered and died, Yea of the 7th had just fallen at the abatis of the Redan, and Laurence of the 2d battalion of the Rifle Brigade, had

* On landing in the Crimea the Light Division was composed as follows :—

1st Brigade, Brigadier Codrington : 7th, 33d, 23d, part Rifle Brigade, Brig.-Maj. Mackenzie.

2d Brigade, Brigadier Butler : 19th, 88th, 77th, part of the Rifle Brigade, Brig.-Maj. G. V. Maxwell.

been sent home at death's door; and nearly all the successors to these commanders had become non-effective from wounds, ill-health, or death.

A pretty catalogue for those who seek renown, the rare prize of fame in the lottery of war; and a lamentable example of the evil of throwing an undue portion of labour on one division only of an army.

At this time the generality of officers commanding companies in the division were inexperienced youths, brave as their swords, but ignorant of the common rudiments of company or battalion formation or movements—of the interior economy, or of the wants and necessities of the soldier. The old experienced sergeants and non-commissioned officers were nearly gone; the enemy, labour, hard work, and sickness had done their work, and the men themselves were composed of raw drafts and levies without a sufficient admixture of soldiers to set an example, to teach the young, to uphold obedience, in a word, to leaven the mass.

Valour without discipline is akin to modesty without clothes; it may be useful to the individual possessor, but it is worthless to the mass. Thus, though the ancient spirit of bravery was implanted in the hearts of our troops (the Light Division), the discipline, the obedience, the teaching, the system, which were requisite to unite the individual spirit, and make the body formidable, were evaporating. The invincible soldiers of the Alma and of Inkerman, formed during peace, and of veteran standing of five, ten, and fifteen years' service, were gone, or almost so, and a skeleton remained of raw, youthful, and inexperienced recruits.

CHAPTER X.

TUESDAY the 19th of June will be remembered as
a most dreary day,—on that day we realised for the
first time the losses of which the generals and other
chief officials had previously been informed.   Not
only in our own division, but in others also, hosts of
old friends and comrades were no more, and amongst
those most generally regretted was Sir John Campbell of the 38th Regiment.

The British loss on the 18th was 85 officers and
1445 men.

Of all the regiments that suffered, the 34th had to
lament the greatest loss. On the 10th of June (Sunday)
this regiment paraded the strongest of the brigade—
eight days subsequently it had scarcely a duty officer left.

Towards the afternoon of the 19th the whole of the troops was ordered under arms for parade—each regiment in front of its respective lines, and a truce was arranged.   The object of the parade was to prevent officers and soldiers going in large parties to the trenches as on previous occasions.   Fatigue parties were detailed from each corps to bring in and bury its dead in the brigade burying-grounds, and close to where we usually formed for parade.

About four P.M. the truce was established and all were immediately busy.   The corpses not recovered directly after they fell, or during the night of the 18th, had now been exposed to the action of the elements for nearly thirty-six hours, and to that of a burning sun for twenty-four, viz., on Monday and Tuesday, so that, as may be readily imagined, the sight was terrible to look upon.   The heat, and the myriads of flies which immediately settled on the gory remains, hastened the process of decomposition, so that many of our friends were scarcely recognisable, so altered had their features become.

Though most of the carpenters from each regiment had been at work, making coffins from such materials as they could procure, the supply was not equal to the demand, and several of the officers' bodies (amongst them that of our late Brigadier Yea, the Colonel of the 7th), were sown in blankets and thus buried, hastily yet solemnly, close to the locality where, in life, they had so often paraded and turned out by day and by night.

After the unfortunate attack on the afternoon of the 18th, the brigade of Guards was brought to the front and encamped a considerable distance to the rear of the second brigade of the Light Division. On the 17th February 1855, the Guards, scarcely three hundred strong, marched down to the neighbourhood of Balaclava, and were subsequently hutted on the hill and slope overlooking the road between that town and the village of Kadikoi. They had now returned, augmented in numbers, in health and strength, but they knew nothing of the intricacies of the trenches, having done no duty there since the first bombardment in October 1854, although they had assisted to break ground on the arrival of the army before the place.

The magnitude of our works was now very great, and the extent of the trenches could be computed by miles. The 72d, lately arrived, was also brought

up and located in the rear of the Fourth Division.
These two corps formed the guards of the trenches on
the night of the 18th, assisted by the 23d, which
had not been engaged.

We who were habitually on duty in the trenches
sometimes made mistakes in threading our way
through them ; it is not therefore to be wondered
at that, in the darkness ignorant of the locales of
zig-zags immediately in their front in taking up
their respective positions, these fresh troops should,
on alarm being raised, have been unaware and completely ignorant that, when firing, their comrades
or brother soldiers would be endangered.   From this
deplorable want of knowledge several soldiers of the
23d were killed on this unfortunate night, for from
some cause confusion arose and a heavy musketry
fire was at once directed upon the spot.

With the French a regular staff was usually detailed for their trenches ; with the British there was
nothing of the sort.   The only members of the staff
obliged to proceed to, or who served a tour of
duty in the trenches, were the brigadiers, in turn
with their aides-de-camp, and even this arrangement
did not commence until after Sir James Simpson's

arrival; he caused some system to be established, and a general to be in command of, and present in, each " attack."

Before that arrangement was made there was, nominally, a general officer in charge of the two attacks, who paid occasional or frequent visits as fancy or sense of duty dictated, but he rarely remained in the trenches. No subordinates from the general staff were detailed for a tour of duty in the trenches, consequently, unless these officers had learned the intricacies in a regimental capacity, they never had an opportunity of studying them on the staff, and were of necessity ignorant of them.

The number of men employed as guards and working parties was between fifteen hundred and eighteen hundred men—the working parties were under the command of a field officer, who divided his men according to the requirements of the engineer on duty; the guards were placed under the orders of a lieutenant-colonel, who had nobody to assist him in the detail except the adjutant on duty, and, as miles separated the extremities of the attack, whilst arrangements were being made on one flank, or on the right or left advance, it frequently happened there was no head to whom to refer at the opposite point.

If the subordinate staff deputy-assistants of the Light and Second Divisions had been placed on a roster,* and each had been obliged in turn to assist the lieutenant-colonel in arranging the detail of visiting the trenches, and been regularly on duty there for the period fixed (whether twelve or twenty-four hours), it would have much lightened a very onerous labour thrown on the shoulders of the commander and his two majors, and would besides have made these young staff officers conversant with the works through which they were supposed to have guided the troops on the 8th of September.

To many the sale of the effects of deceased officers or soldiers after an action is most painful. Should the late owner happen to have been a messmate, or an intimate comrade, the very articles put up seem to be part of himself. After the affair of the 18th of

* A military term signifying a list according to seniority for the duties of the rank to which those entered belong. Opposite each name the date of the last tour of duty is placed, and the officer's turn cannot again come on until every name on this list has a later date of a tour of duty opposite it. Of course sickness prevents the discharge of the duty, in which case the word " sick " instead of the date is affixed.

June each regiment held its own auction, the hour proposed being made known throughout the division and adjacent camps.

Much depended of course on the skill of the auctioneer, who generally was a serjeant, but it was usual to sell everything except perhaps the deceased man's sword, Bible, watch, or other trifles—these, according as the taste or the discretion of the members of the board of three officers decided, were kept and sent home. Everything else was offered, bid for, and knocked down as expeditiously as possible.

Many sales were held during the last ten days of June 1855. When we consider that most of the articles put up to auction might have been bought new at the wooden stores at Kadikoi, and further, as, from the many sales going on in every part of the camp, the market was quite overstocked, yet the prices fetched were surprising. In some cases double the original cost was paid. A saddle rarely went below the sum at which it might have been bought in the shop, but more frequently it was sold for a third more. The same with bridles; bits, and a curry comb with brush, judging from the bidding, must

have been rare and much sought-for articles. Jams,
boots, plates, sheets, and bedding were also in great
request. The three first items invariably produced
very lively and active bidding. Without remorse
the very penates of one's best friend were put up for
the "best friend" to buy or bid for; and as numerous
wants arise at the sight of luxuries, it often happened
the "best friend" heard the auctioneer's knock that
proclaimed him the fortunate possessor with any
other feelings than those of compunction.

It is a very wholesome and proper regulation
which obliges the effects of deceased officers and soldiers to be sold. How otherwise could they be
disposed of? The value, or more than the value, is
realised by the auction, and the money is then re-
mitted to the War Department in the paymaster's
accounts.

The maimed and wounded were taken in a con-
tinual stream from the front to the ships at Kamiesch,
and Balaclava, or to the hospital near the latter. A
few also found their way to the neighbourhood of the
Monastery of St George, for the benefit of change of
air. Men who, a few weeks previously had been in
robust health and activity, might be seen in all

directions pale, emaciated, hobbling about, perhaps
lopped of a limb, and in many instances so weak
and nervous as to be utterly helpless.

It is curious to observe how susceptible and nervous a wounded man becomes who, previously to
his hurt, might be said to have no such thing as
nerves. There were many patients, some seriously,
some slightly injured, unable to rest, whose recovery
would have been retarded by the noise and appre-
hension of the enemy's fire had they been allowed to
remain at the front. A feeling of insecurity and
helplessness was begotten, and dread of a successful
sortie was the uppermost thought.

Not merely was this the accompaniment in one
case, but it was so with most of the wounded, and
the noise of the musketry, and the voices or shouts
of the combatants became at length quite a torture.
Of course the doctors, for the sake of better food
and change of air, were desirous of removing their
suffering patients. Accordingly conveyances for
their transport daily arrived.

The vehicles were astounding contrivances! But
that they were here, it is scarcely possible to believe
that any official, possessing a grain of fellow feeling

for suffering humanity, could have seen one of them
prior to exportation.   They were in shape something
like a hearse, and the living body was slid in at the
back much in the manner of a corpse.   They were
without springs, or with springs so stiff and of such
a rude description, that their very action was worse
than no spring at all.   In the centre of the hearse-
shaped conveyance was an upright division, on each
side of which slides were made, so that tiers of
stretchers were slid in one above the other.

On these the mutilated or suffering bodies were
placed.   The process of loading was as follows : the
vehicle drew 'up awkwardly, with risk of over-
turning, and the postilions, a hybrid class, neither
exactly combatant nor civilian, dismounted.   The
ponderous doors behind were unfastened and opened,
when the required number of stretchers was slid out
and taken to the hospital marquee or hut, where a
patient was laid on each, and returning, was successively slid, or rather shot into, the interior of
the conveyance.   The packs and arms of the inmates
were stored, and the door of the hind boot was then
shut.

All this time a magnificent-looking mounted officer

viewed the process, interfering only when the load
was complete.   He was the subordinate officer in
charge ; when all was ready he gave the word of
command, and started off leading the cortège at
a round trot, shaking, bruising, and torturing the
helpless cargo inside.

It has been sometimes the lot of inventors of instruments for torture or for death to suffer by their
own inventions.   Guillotine died under the knives
of the guillotine, his invention bearing his own
name ; and the peer reputed to have introduced the
" maiden," expiated by its means the cruelty of his
invention.   To those who furnished the army of the
Crimea with these ambulances, the lightest punishment they should be called upon to suffer should be,
to be driven therein over some ten miles of rough
country.   Then, immovable in a stretcher as if in a
strait waistcoat, the body dashed one way, the head
knocked against the wood above, the agonising voices
unheard by the driver, without air to breathe, or
with sufficient dust mixed therein to stifle and choke
the patient—the healthy person of the inventor
would be able to appreciate the possible intense
agony and sufferings of the sick or wounded

when borne away in this triumph of inexperience.

When the war first broke out our theorists at the War Office, at a loss what to provide and yet unwilling to leave the matter in the hands of the military, called for the opinion of a much-abused head of the medical department in the first instance, when some very sensible proposals were made.

Unfortunately there was a power greater than theirs. There was one individual who, having been a volunteer in the Burmah War of 1825-6, had earned a commission, and now, *without ever having served one hour on full pay beyond the rank of subaltern,* he had, through the influence of successive Secretaries for War, been promoted on the half-pay list from captain to colonel, and in this rank was attached to the War Department. His career was singular. Without ability to take a position in the senior department of the Military College at Sandhurst, he yet contrived to crawl through, and subsequently, by the study of statistics and with the assistance of others, he propounded a plan to Government for the organisation and payment of pensioners, which was adopted.

No sooner was the subject of the ambulances broached than he claimed the sanction of the then Secretary at War, not only to build conveyances under his own superintendence, but to organise a corps for their management and to attend on the sick and wounded.   As originally arranged, the corps was formed of old pensioners, who, having been some years discharged, were enjoying their pension (generally of a shilling a day), with "otium cum dignitate," unrestrained by any trammels of military discipline. Many of these were now called upon for active duty as members of the ambulance corps.

It is not difficult for a deserving pensioner discharged with a good character, and tolerably hale, after residing some time in a country village, to obtain a small post on the railway or in his parish. These men were, generally speaking, content ; but the worthless and abandoned, tempted by the high pay offered, eagerly adopted this new branch of the service opened to them, and at once joined the ranks.

The result was not long in showing itself.   Before even the landing in the Crimea, whilst the army was still in Bulgaria, the corps was decimated by its utter want of discipline and gross irregularities, and

N

excessive sickness preying on worn-out frames was
the consequent result.

When the distresses of the winter of 1854-5
afflicted the army before Sebastopol, its corps of
ambulance attendants was all but helpless. In vain
did its originator pen letter after letter to its unfortunate local commandant, extolling the arrangements
but finding fault with him for not rendering a better
account of the regiment. At last its unfortunate
officer was forced to represent to Lord Raglan's staff
at head quarters, that it was utterly impossible to
continue any longer as a corps the miserable remains
of what was once the ambulance of the British army.

The stories about the men (old pensioners) selected
exceed belief if they were not vouched for by indis-
putable authority. On one occasion in the bad times
an ambulance was driven and conducted by the sick
soldiers who ought to have been its occupants, but
the occupants were the pensioners who should have
been the drivers and attendants, but they were so
drunk they had taken the places of the sick.

This notable scheme was shortly afterwards abandoned, and volunteers called for. But could that
type of all that is amiable, of charity, of philanthropy,

of honest public-spirited kindness, the Right Honourable Sidney Herbert, have known the cruelties inflicted, and the miseries undergone by the maimed and wounded from free scope having been given to that self-sufficient officer who was at that time absolute with the War Office authorities on the subject of military equipment and essentials, and who originated the ambulances, the narrow compartments, and the notable corps, his noble spirit would have been visited with pain and remorse that, on the "ipse dixit" of certain predecessors, he should have blindly trusted a man with the title of "Colonel," but who possessed no further qualification for his post than the ignorance and inexperience of a recruit.

CHAPTER XI.

CONCLUSION.

Final Attack on Sebastopol Marred from Want of Knowledge by Officers of the Staff — Red-tapeism and Disastrous Results— Culpable Return of the Brigadier from the Redan—A Pernicious Example—Death of Lord Raglan—The Fables of Æsop—Peace Proclaimed—The Casualties and Costs of War—Superiority of the British Army.

THE finale of the taking of Sebastopol is now thoroughly well known. The plan of the attack was well arranged. As soon as the stormers had advanced against the salient of the Redan, the supports were immediately to jump over the parapet of their trenches and run across the open to the fifth parallel, the troops in the third parallel to the fourth, and so on successively, but this plan, so well digested in theory was abandoned in practice and entirely marred by some officers of the staff who were wholly ignorant of the intricacies of the trenches, and consequently utterly incompetent to discharge the momentous duties entrusted to them in this supreme movement.

Whether through superior authority and orders, or from individual self-sufficiency is unknown, but the supports and reserves, instead of going out as in-

tended, went meandering down the zig-zags and
trenchways in single file. In fine weather and the
most peaceful times it took upwards of two hours to
reach the advanced trench in this manner when relieving the guards—it may therefore easily be understood, when the banquettes were crowded and the
trenches choked with killed and wounded, how long
a time, and with what great difficulty a regiment
could make its way along. Yet Indian file was the
mode adopted, and consequently it is a fact that, on
debouching from the trenches, the rear companies of
several regiments were wholly ignorant of what had
become of their leading companies.

Young staff-officers, too, were sent to show the way,
to lead officers who, having been nightly on duty,
well knew the works and only required to be told
the position where they and their troops were
wanted; even some of the staff-officers sent to lead
were constrained and not ashamed to enquire the
proper route of those they were presumed to direct.

Good, however, as the plan of the attack originally
and undoubtedly was, it was directed to one single
point only, whereas, if there had been several false
attacks at the same time under determined leaders,

the attention of the enemy would have been diverted and distracted ; in addition, as chances might turn out, these false attacks would possibly have been changed into real and substantial successes.

Having once gained a footing in the Redan, our retirement therefrom is a rare and unfortunate feature in our annals. Various circumstances combined to cause this, and there cannot be a doubt that the horror inspired by the reports widely spread of the fougasse or mine existing in the fortress greatly operated to prevent the majority of the troops making a determined advance and charge. Want of supports was another reason, but the crowning event leading to the catastrophe was unquestionably the sight of the brigadier going back, no matter from what cause.

Public opinion and the country having made a hero of the man who, having gained a firm footing in the enemy's work, went back *in person* to seek reinforcements, it may be thought presumption on our part to canvass this act of the leader. Yet amongst military men there can be but one opinion on the subject. It may be laid down as an unchangeable axiom, if a body of troops see their leader go, or being carried, to the rear their joint

efforts are weakened, but if the majority of the men
fighting see their leader, unhurt, turn his back to the
enemy, it is very certain the men will quickly follow
such a pernicious example,—and it cannot be matter
for surprise. The soldier, taught to look up first
to the leader of his squad, then to the captain of
his company whose very aspect or dumb movement
ought to carry confidence and tacit obedience, in a far
greater ratio still beholds every act of his commander.
For this very reason doubtless many great commanders,
when mortally wounded, have concealed their wounds,
or have directed that their disasters should be kept quiet.

So in the navy: if the admiral falls in action his
flag is still kept flying in order to avoid a pre-
judicial feeling arising from the knowledge of a
leader's death, and thus prevent the panic that
might otherwise result.

A wholesome regulation! Hitherto in the British
army when a sergeant, a captain, a colonel, or other
leader has been compelled to turn his back to the
enemy and to retire, he has usually chosen to be the
last man to leave, and not the first. And though
posterity may pause in admiration of the cool and
thoughtful words of the gallant Windham (uttered

to an officer of the 90th Foot) when he went to the rear to seek supports, experienced military men will not fail to condemn the act itself, evincing as it did utter ignorance of the feelings that assist to guide the troops, and betraying a want of knowledge of the commonest principle that directs mankind in general—the force of example.

The wound we had received on the 18th of June, piercing as it did the leg in which we were already maimed, necessitated our removal from active duty, and eventually led to our being ordered home. In the meantime the siege progressed with increased energy, the crisis evidently rapidly drawing near.

But that crisis was heralded by a great national calamity. Lord Raglan, who had nobly done his work and had gathered fresh laurels to entwine around his country's crown, was not destined to witness the complete success of his long and toilsome labour. On June 28th, 1855, he succumbed to an attack, it is said, of diarrhœa, followed by cholera. His decease took the army and the nation by surprise, casting over all a gloom that did not quickly disappear. On 3d July his remains were placed on board H.M.S. Caradoc, then lying in Kazatch Bay,—on the same

evening she sailed for England, and General Simpson
succeeded to the command by virtue of seniority.

Events now followed each other with considerable
rapidity—Sweaborg was bombarded on the 9th of
August ; another attempt of the Russians in the
Tchernaya valley on the 16th of August to change
the aspect of affairs was wholly defeated ; early in
September the French seized the Malakoff, and kept
possession of it to the end, whilst the assault of the
English on the Redan was unsuccessful.   Here, lying
by the side of an abandoned gun, a Russian illustrated
copy of the Fables of Æsop was picked up.   It
was very quaint, the illustrations rude in character, in the style of the wood blocks first used
after wood-engraving was invented.   It was evidently the literary companion of the gunner, and,
poring over its pages, maybe his attention was
arrested by the fable of " The Fox and the Grapes,"
—looking with a longing eye to the country of the
Turk, he probably fled from his gun in disgust, feeling
in his inmost soul, " Verily the grapes are sour."

At this time also the enemy sunk or destroyed the
remainder of his fleet in the harbour, and retired to
the forts on the north of the city.   On the 9th of

September the allied forces entered and took possession of Sebastopol, which they retained till the following July, having in the month of April wholly blown up and destroyed all the works of the docks and arsenal. In November the Czar visited his army, again retiring to St Petersburg, and in the same month General Simpson resigned his command to Sir William Codrington. In December Austria made proposals of peace to the Czar, which were accepted subject to a Conference of the nations, and which opened at Paris on February 25, 1856 ; on the 2d April peace was proclaimed in the Crimea, but not in London till the 29th of the same month,— by the middle of July the Crimea was evacuated.

Composed almost wholly of recruits, as the Light Division of the Crimean army was at the time of the final assault, on the 8th September, with scarcely any leaven of old soldiers, it is to be regretted that some of the regiments of veterans belonging to the Third Division were not employed. And though the regiments of the Light Division were a mere skeleton of what they originally were at the commencement of the war, the same gallant spirit that had animated their fallen comrades still prevailed.

Immediately after the war the time was mostly devoted to disciplining the troops, and instructing them, *ab initio,* in the full knowledge of their profession as soldiers, and this was not without great and lasting benefit, the fruits of which, in some of these corps, may now be seen in India and elsewhere, where their readiness to uphold the honour of their country is most marked, exemplifying the motto, *aucto splendore resurgo.*

The losses sustained by the countries engaged in the war cannot be stated with accuracy, but that they were enormously heavy does not admit of doubt—the arms of precision employed, the strength, calibre, and number of the guns and mortars, coupled with the daring of the men and the obstinate tenacity with which they fought on every occasion when fair fighting was permitted, and the length of the siege easily explain this.   It is computed that we lost in killed, wounded, by disease, and other casualites about thirty thousand men ; whilst the addition of the cost added to the national debt was nearly £50,000,000.   The French losses amounted to about sixty-five thousand men ; whilst the loss of the foe is computed at not less certainly than five hundred thousand men. The costs incurred it is utterly impossible to estimate.

We cannot close our narrative without expressing our belief, after our experiences in the Crimean campaign, that when the British soldier is led by officers of experience and courage in whom he has confidence, there is no post of danger where he will not follow his leader, and no troops he will not willingly meet though in much greater numbers than his own; and further, there is no army in the world, man for man and officer for officer, that can be compared for a moment with the troops constituting the British forces.

That Great Britain may long maintain her position and influence in the councils of Europe on behalf of oppressed nationalities, christian or otherwise; that she may never cast her sword into the scales on behalf of any cause, country or crown, unworthy her support; and that, wherever just and righteous cause can be shown she will be ever ready to unsheathe her sword and do battle nobly, vigorously and triumphantly in that cause is our most earnest prayer.